OUT OF RED DIRT
(AND UP COWBELL HILL)

a collection of growing-up stories from the
Oklahoma riverbeds to the Colorado Rockies

authored by sue nell phillips
published: fall, 2012

OUT OF RED DIRT
(AND UP COWBELL HILL)

This is a work of creative nonfiction. Some details and dialogue have been invented or embellished, but all stories maintain the integrity of the original actions and words of the persons herein. A few names have been altered to protect the innocent and guilty. ☺

ISBN-13: 978-1478394273

Oh give me a home where the buffalo roam,
Where the deer and the antelope play,
Where seldom is heard, a discouraging word,
And the skies are not cloudy all day...

Dedicated to all
present and future Streets and Phillipses,
wherever they may roam

TABLE OF CONTENTS

-1-

I AM. . .

"Now I lay me down to
I pray the Lord my soul to keep,
If I should die before I wake ...Who me?"

tom phillips street
age three

I am red dirt, acorns and elm trees, and "little lambs eat ivy"
under the bay window, bubbly black tar on Guilford Lane,
rainwater rushing over my legs in the gutter under pouring July
skies.

I am sixty-four frilly dresses, a pink diaper on a post in the
front yard which reads, "It's a girl!", a doll in a slave's cradle on
wheels surrounded by four "adoring brothers" in the Daily
Oklahoman.

I am the youngest and smallest and only girl, playing with
Chatty Kathy next to the dollhouse beside the mirror, red
lipstick smeared on my mouth, beneath a pile of pin curls, all

dressed up in pink organdy…and later, ironing in my apron, red pinafore, and snappy, black patent leather shoes.

I am stealing a second Krackle bar out of Mrs. Cramer's refrigerator or bubble gum at the drugstore that "of course" I paid for when my brother Bill asks, or perhaps siphoning off a bit of change not yet turned in after trick-or-treating for UNICEF, later replenished with all my money saved for Christmas presents. Mother refused to double it that year.

I am eating lemon drops from the tin in Nanny's sewing chest, the one next to the back door, and Daddy's black licorice, which I try once or twice or thrice and always end up spitting out with my puckered lips and squenched up nose.

Or it's Christmastime, so I scale the chairs that "Nell never did like anyway" onto Nanny's dining room table where I always find curly hard candies, striped and painted with little crimson and yellow flowers…but only at Christmastime.

Then it's summer, and Papa comes in with "stwaberries" from beyond the fence. In a twinkling, they are washed and topped and circling a sweet mound of sugar crystals which, after dipping, and licking and sighing, paint my lips and chin red and wet and sticky beneath my contented smile.

I am the youngest and smallest and only girl, whether in the backyard with the entire neighborhood playing Mother May

I, Red Light-Green Light, or Punch the Nose on the Icebox, crocodile tears streaming down my cheeks, "No I can't count to a hundred!", or in the front yard watching Bill and Richard Lee, Peter Hoffman and the Lisle boys, and all the others playing football in Hoffman's yard because it's flat with no weeds, unlike ours.

I am the youngest and smallest and only girl with seven tense grandsons around the roasted turkey and the cranberry sherbet for cleansing the palate, and Granddaddy Street at the head; Granddaddy who will decide the "sayer of grace" this year. (He dies before it falls on me, the youngest and smallest and only girl.)

It's Sunday night and I am watching "Sing Along with Mitch" and Lawrence Welk in Nanny's kitchen, or welcoming Ed Sullivan into the sitting room at Grandmother Street's before an evening of cards with the Adams, the Hargetts, and others; and I get to serve the ice water from the left and pick up from the right.

I am the mayor's only granddaughter and, from his car, can barely see a young, handsome, Catholic war hero speaking at a campaign rally. Nixon and Kennedy buttons are on all the lapels around town (mostly Nixon, of course), but Mom sure does like Jackie, her hats and her smart, tailored suits. I see her again and again in the ensuing months as Mother flips from back to front through *Vogue, Good Housekeeping* and *Better Homes and Garden.* And there she is again in her hat and tailored suit in a convertible, waving, and then with red stains on her skirt. A few hours pass and she's next to a Mr. Johnson raising his right hand, and, in only a few days, beside a small boy saluting a flag-draped casket and a riderless horse with the stirrups turned backwards. Everyone is crying…even those with the Nixon buttons on their lapels.

I am three years old and walking down the hill and through the Indian paintbrush and by a Colorado Rocky Mountain columbine or two to the back of SINN'S Western Trail on Highway 7, right across from the post office, 80510. (Well, not yet because there isn't any 80510, but there will be soon.) I march right in and say to Mrs. SINN, "My parents want me to have those beautiful little white cowboy boots," and she says, "Oh really? Are you sure?" "Oh yes, I'm sure. Just put them on our account." And so I walk, or stumble or crawl (cuz as everyone knows, it's a bit difficult to walk in cowboy boots) back up the hill to the cabin. I swing open the screen door and show Mother and Daddy my beautiful new little white cowboy boots that I just put on their account, and somehow, I get away with it. (Perhaps because I am the youngest and smallest and only girl.)

Later Daddy and I go on our first hike of the summer all the way up Cowbell Hill, or at least all the way to the Henry house, that is. (The Henrys whom we don't even know, but later we will and as a matter of fact, my little boy Ryan will take his first steps on their sandstone patio while Gramps has his beer and Nan her white wine.) The Henry house becomes their own after the propane tank blows and Nan singes her eyebrows and the fire eats up the whole house on Willow creek, even with four feet of snow on the ground and roof. But Nan and Gramps and Delilah are safe, so that's all that counts. Bryce and Ryan and I help Gramps live out his last three months on Cowbell Hill before cancer takes over too much of him and he has to move on.

But long before that, Daddy and I go fishin' on Fox with the worms we dug on Rock, followed by a ride on Ranger along Ski Road, or over the backside of Cowbell Hill to the abandoned mine, or to the Old Outcamp that Gramps built when he was a boy and then rebuilt each summer with Jack, Jimmy, Tommy, Bill, and me. And we do all that again every summer, and then we circle the Old Cabin in our station wagon (but this time I'm packed inside the car instead of in a trunk that Jack threw up on the top when Mother and Daddy weren't there and then drove round and round with me in it screaming) and we all yell, "Goodbye Old Cabin! Goodbye Allenspark! See you again next year!" and then we drive all the way back to Oklahoma City in one day because when you're going home you just want to get there. And then you smell August in Oklahoma and hear the cicadas and see the fireflies and feel the air and you know it's really all over again for another year.

And soon I'm "now-I-lay-me-down-to-sleepin'" and I'm beggin', "Say it again Mommy, say it one more time," and Mommy says, "I love you very much, yes indeed I do," (O.K., maybe she said that to Tommy, but I wish she'd said it to me) and after five or ten or so more times the eyelids begin to close on the youngest and smallest and only girl.

-2-

A MEMORIAL
IN PERPETUITY

*Oklahoma! Where the wind comes sweeping down the plain,
And the wavin' wheat can sure smell sweet when the wind
comes right behind the rain!*

Oklahoma State Song

Anemic, black nylon socks dusted with dry skin, ten inches
below the hem of a well-worn nightshirt, shuffle out of a back
hall bedroom each afternoon at four o'clock. Granddaddy Street
awakens from his mandatory mid-afternoon nap and then
makes his way to the kitchen for what I imagine to be a
prescribed medicinal elixir: a warm purée of boiled custard, or
its disappointing substitute, a tall glass of buttermilk. His
vestments, pace, and choice of beverage make it difficult for
me to believe he once was one of the dominant voices and
most flamboyant faces of Oklahoma politics in the twentieth
century.

My Granddaddy Street, "Little Allen," crossed the frontier into Oklahoma in 1891 from Mexia, Texas. It was barely a year after the Sooners jumped the gun before the Land Run of 1889 to stake their claim to theretofore Indian territory. At age six, he could hardly foresee that one day he would follow in his father's, Joseph Gray Street's, enterprising footsteps.

After joining the confederate forces at only fifteen, the elder Street, Joseph Gray, studied medicine in Atlanta, doctored in Tennessee, abandoned the practice of medicine by age twenty-nine, headed south and west peddling pharmaceuticals, then mysteriously switched trades once again to build and sell furniture. For a brief and perhaps infamous year, he served as headmaster of the School for Indian Girls of the Chickasaw Nation, a position that, we can only hope, challenged his moral sensitivities. Fortunately, J.G. Street moved on to business owner and founding father of Oklahoma City. In 1926, by official proclamation of the governor, the entire state and city government came to a halt so all could attend his funeral.

At age ten, his son, Little Allen, began his entrepreneurial and political careers by herding cattle from the backyards of homesteaders to the outskirts of town on ground that would soon lie beneath the Capitol of the forty-sixth state of the Union. Before school and again after the final bell, Allen and his brother Joe led the herd back and forth for a dollar a month per head, not bad pay for a ten-year-old in 1895.

As part of the first graduating class of thirty-one at Oklahoma City High School, his reputation firmly established as both class humorist and manager (of athletic teams, that is), Granddaddy headed off for two years to study at Vanderbilt in his father's home state of Tennessee. He returned in 1907 to Oklahoma City and joined his father in a soon-to-be flourishing business: Street and Draper Funeral Home. (Furniture-making led to casket-making; caskets being the final pieces of furniture purchased this side of paradise, purgatory,...or hell.)

Oklahomans were a fiery bunch of ruffians in the early years of the 1900's, resulting in a higher than average demand for services and burials. After taking note of the number of robberies, murders, brothels, and barroom brawls, a visiting evangelist from Tulsa noted, "Since my visit to Oklahoma City, I am confirmed in my belief that hell was made too little from the start."

Sensing a rising demand for his services, Joseph Gray Street offered up one of his furniture stores as a morgue, became the county coroner, and joined with J.M. Draper to found the "undertaking parlor" that would support three generations of Oklahoma Streets. One-half of Granddaddy's career was set.

The other half, the political one, was drawing to a close in 1958 when his granddaughter, that would be me, cut the ribbon for the opening of Wedgewood Amusement Park in northwest Oklahoma City, my only official duty in support of his thirty-six year political career.

It began with a defeat in 1923. At age thirty-eight, he lost his first mayoral race to Otto Cargill. Humbled, he took his sights off the executive branch and sought a seat in the state legislature where he served five terms and became Speaker of the House in 1928. In 1943, he moved to the City Council, and finally took over the city helm in 1947. Three terms and $68.6 million in municipal bonds later, I cut the final ribbon of his illustrious career.

***

Granddaddy laughed loudly, wore a bow tie below his enormous grin, and delighted in scratching the tender cheeks of his seven grandchildren with his late-in-the-day shadow each time we came for a visit. The ritual was clearly more for his amusement than out of any affection for us. All seven dreaded those greetings as much as a bully's gauntlet on the way to class.

The training which followed his greeting included: standing when someone older entered the room, grasping their hand with a firm politician's handshake, looking them straight in the eye, and punctuating responses with "yes, sir" and "yes, ma'am." He persevered in instilling the latter with a five cent per response bribe, but with disproportionate success. He was, however, pleased with my progress in perfecting "lady-like" manners, inviting me to serve ice water to his card-playing cronies once a month on Sunday evening in the formal dining room.

Granddaddy suffered a heart attack in his early fifties—a mild one for sure—but one which shaped the rest of his years. He moved from the three-story Tudor on McKinley where he and Grandmother had hosted many guests at dances and teas in the third-floor ballroom, to a more modest, one-story home on Thirty-Eighth Street with no stairs to strain his engine.

He gave up driving—no doubt a blessing for all concerned since he frequently took out the stone porch steps when backing down the driveway of the McKinley home, his funeral-black coupe leaving behind much mortar and many dents.

The heart attack also initiated a reduced workday at Street and Draper and the afternoon nap. Dad would pick him up on the way to the office in the morning, where he generally proved himself a nuisance, and Grandmother Street would chauffeur him home again for lunch and, as he said, "to lie down for just a bit."

On Sundays, after church at Westminster Presbyterian where he proudly wore his charter member pin, we dropped him across the street from Oklahoma City Golf and Country Club. He'd make his way slowly across Pennsylvania Avenue with a limp and a cane; not for tennis, a swim, or a swing, but for pinochle with other city founders.

My mother and dad ascribed to him more than a small bit of hypochondria. That, no doubt, contributed to a grandson's response when Granddaddy exclaimed during a trip to Arizona, "My heart has stopped beating!" Thirteen-year-old Jimmy responded, "Granddaddy, you must be dead!"

Nonetheless, Granddaddy Street cast a bright and celebrated light in Oklahoma City society. His legislative career was acclaimed by then Governor Murray, who asserted, "Allen Street is the most economical man in the house of the thirteenth legislature!" While his son, Gordon, my father, usually addressed humorous, impious letters home to his grandmother McElhiney and his mother, Mary Erma (where he described factual and fictional adventures at Cheley Camps, boarding school, and the U.S. Naval Academy), he knew who had the *real* power and influence. After his graduation, when he was threatened with dismissal from the Navy for marrying Nell Carpenter Phillips before the one year mandatory waiting period, he wrote to his father for help—to no avail, I might add. The Pentagon bureaucracy was not as taken by Granddaddy's grin and handshake as his Oklahoma colleagues.

When Granddaddy's older son, Bob Allen Street, died tragically at a young thirty-one years, Granddaddy gave a building in his memory to the Oklahoma Council of the Boy Scouts of America to serve as Council headquarters. He re-entered politics and ran for mayor to continue the contributions that Bob Allen and his earlier deceased daughter, Mary Louise, would have made to the city. He served as local, district, and national president of Rotary Club and narrowly missed being elected Rotary International president—the scuttlebutt being that his funereal profession, not generally admired in Europe, brought him down. The city he served honored him with a bust and a building at the Myriad Center in downtown Oklahoma City, a building later re-named for a younger city philanthropist—how quickly we are forgotten—especially when all the namesakes flee the honoree's hometown.

By far the foremost memorial to Granddaddy Street does not stand, however, in a building in Oklahoma City. It lies in a pit in the most remote recesses of his grandchildren's stomachs. We are gathered around a finely set, multi-leaf mahogany table, covered in white linen and Christmas holly. We are clad in polished wing-tips and patent-leather, choking ties and scratchy petticoats, starched dress-shirts and Florence Eiseman pinafores. Before us rest gold-rimmed goblets of cranberry ice, and from the kitchen, aromas tease and tantalize our impatient palates.

But we wait. We squirm. We keep our heads bowed, somehow hoping we'll escape the twinkling eyes and Polident grin commanding the head of the table:

Granddaddy Street.

He is, no doubt, aware of the power he holds over us and the anxiety he calls forth each December twenty-fourth. What we're all awaiting, anticipating, and dreading, of course, is his pronouncement. His gaze glides from crown to crown, from pin curls to widow's peak. Then, "Tommy..." He pauses for full effect, "Will you say the blessing for us this year?"

It's not really a question--it's a sentencing, and the rest of us breathe the sigh of proverbial reprieve. The blessing is a blur, but the "Amen!" is hearty and heart-felt. We clean our palates and then dive into the turkey, stuffing, spiced peaches and pumpkin pie.

2 A MEMORIAL IN PERPETUITY

Yet, almost immediately, the seeds of anxiety take root once again for a full bloom the following Christmas Eve—a memorial in perpetuity to Granddaddy Street.

HOOKY

"So this is where I find you! How do you expect to become a real boy?...You're comin' home with me right this minute!"

Jiminy Cricket

"A juvenile delinquent, that's what Buddy is."

All the mothers at *The Little Playhouse* seemed to agree—only problem, he was only three.

Buddy was forever being punished, banished from our fellowship for some onerous misdeed, while the rest of us three-year-olds sat crossed-legged in a circle and sang,

Come to the Playhouse and we'll have fun
Boys and girls together, joy for everyone...
Playhouse, Little Playhouse, the house that was built
with love.

I'm not sure Buddy felt much love or joy, especially the day he threw up in his own shirt as he sat in a doll's bed, atoning for his latest criminal act. He had been sent there by Mrs. Mann who had already lost hope for him. I think my mother had, too.

Buddy was in our carpool. He lived right down the street from Cindy Upshire, known as Cindy "Downshire" by my brothers, and around the corner from Becky Flint. I remember well the day that Buddy slipped out of the car when we got to Jimmy Barber's house. While Mother paused to chat with Mrs. Barber, Buddy jumped out the door on the other side of the car. A few moments later, Mother tucked herself in behind the wheel, so as not to wrinkle her skirt, and began to count,

"One, two, three, four, five…whoops, no five. Who's missing?" she said.

Before anyone could tattle, she stepped out of the car and locked her eyes on Buddy. He danced around with fingers in his ears and a "neh, neh, neh, neh, neh" grin. My mother was neither amused nor flustered. I had never seen her lose control in my five long years, and this was not to be the day.

"Buddy, get back in the car," she said, her voice even and low.

"No!"

We surveyed one another with sideways glances. *Who was she kidding?*

"Buddy, we are leaving now. Get in the car." She marched toward the back of the station wagon.

Buddy circled ahead of her, slinging another challenge over his shoulder, "No!"

My mother was quick to recognize the imminent game of "Mulberry Bush." She turned, paused to breathe deeply, walked unremarkably to her open door, slid behind the wheel, smoothed her skirt yet again, checked her lipstick in the rearview mirror, and began to back up.

At first, Buddy thought she was only toying with him. He took off down the street, glancing occasionally over his shoulder, intending to enjoy her exasperation. He was disappointed. Soon he could hear the change of gears and squeaking tires as she set off towards *The Little Playhouse*, eyes and hands firmly fixed. The last we saw of him as we turned our heads, all together, was an open mouth and dropped jaw, reflecting our own.

I guess Jimmy's mom rounded up Buddy and hauled him home. Later in the day his mother called, desperate and pleading, "*What* can I *do* with him?"

I'm sure she thought wise advice was forthcoming from a mother of four boys. Mother, however, cool like dry ice, responded, "If you don't know how to control your own three-year-old son, don't ask me."

***

So why my mother ever let me go over and play with Buddy that morning before kindergarten, I'll never know. Perhaps it was part of her method of training me for adulthood; allowing me to make wise, independent choices. I was five, after all. Or perhaps she was due at her Sewing Club, where no one ever sewed.

For my part, there had been no better offers, and perhaps Buddy represented that tiny piece of me that yearned to scream, "No!" instead of the obedient, "Yes, m-ma'am" that typically trembled from my tender lips. In any case, off I went to Buddy's house in my saddle shoes, green and red plaid jumper, and double pony tails. I carried my *Pinocchio* board game under my arm.

The morning's activities draw a blank for me. They must have been pretty innocent because I seem to remember vividly all the trespasses in my life, a consequence of my mother's back-of-the-head eyes.

Around eleven o'clock, Buddy's mom packed us a sack lunch and sent us off to the park to share our PB & J's and chocolate chip cookies, and then head for Nichols Hills Elementary School. I still had the *Pinocchio* game in tow since I would walk home after the three o'clock bell.

All went well at first. We ate a few bites and then Buddy suggested the teeter totter. I was a bit reticent; Buddy had not proven most trustworthy on this piece of equipment. Just the week before he had devilishly let me down too fast, intentionally smashing into the red dirt of the schoolyard and sending me over the top of the handle on the opposite end where my forehead met the board with a *smack!* But I was a forgiving sort, still eager to give Buddy a chance. I climbed on the long end and up I went. He was a perfect gentleman.

It was nearing noon when I reminded Buddy that we had best pack up and be on our way so as to arrive at school before the tardy bell.

"Ah, neh. We've got plenty of time," he assured me. "Let's play *Pinocchio*. Let's just stay at the park and play *Pinocchio* all afternoon. We can head home when we hear the closing bell..." (We weren't more than four blocks from the school) "...and no one will ever know."

I don't know why I wasn't more shocked or morally outraged by this astonishing suggestion. It sounded fairly reasonable, and a lot more fun than painting stars or practicing the *Hokey Pokey* with kids who didn't know their left from their right.

I don't actually remember saying, "O.K.," but before I knew it, we had the board out of the box and, just like in the storybook, we were on the road somewhere between Gepetto's toy shop and the two hoodlums who intoxicated us with movies and candy and a trip to Pleasure Island. Of course, I wanted to become a real little boy, but I kept drawing cards that said I had told a lie and my nose grew longer and longer and before I knew it, I was caged.

Hoping to draw a green card that would set me free, instead, I heard a faint voice above the giggles and "It's your turns." Maybe it was Jiminy Cricket, or maybe it was the bell that suddenly invaded the land of bad little boys and girls. My heart leapt like Jiminy out of my chest and my cheeks sizzled with shame. Maybe this wasn't such a great idea after all.

"Let's g-g- go," I said, my lower lip stuttering with remorse.

"Wimp! Scaredy cat! Sucker!" Buddy said, but my heart was beating too fast and too loud to hear. The seconds were ticking toward the tardy bell and I wanted to be in my classroom.

I hastened to pack away the cards and dice and little plastic *Pinocchio* pieces, despite the complaints and chiding and rolling eyes of Buddy.

But then it happened. It came across the rooftops, around a couple of corners, and through the trees.

Brrrrrring!

The second bell. And I was playing hooky in the park with Buddy Carr. And I was only in kindergarten. I scrambled up, confused.

"It's too late," Buddy said, trying to tie his shoe. "We're already tardy. Let's just stay here. Let's see who can swing the highest. I'll race you. Last one there's a rotten egg!"

It was tempting. Why face all those glaring eyes and questions, the humiliation, and maybe...a whooping?

I'd had one once before when I knocked my mother's checkbook off the counter at TG & Y when she'd just begun to write the date. I have no idea why I did it. This overwhelming desire robbed me of all rational thought. I wasn't mad—or anything. The checkbook flew off the counter and slid across the linoleum tiles. The shock on the checker's face, echoing on my own, was excelled only by my mother's embarrassment. I knew immediately that I was in trouble, trouble unlike any I'd ever known before.

My mother didn't speak to me all the way home. She just let me twist in the clutches of voiceless terror. I suffered. I truly, repentantly, suffered.

When we got home, she told me to get out of the car. Then she offered me a choice: "Do you want me to spank you out here or inside?" she said, hairbrush in hand.

My four older brothers and their friends were playing football in the Hoffman's yard across the street. They would all see me.

"I don't care!" I fired. The words jettisoned through my clenched jaw from who knows where and why. I couldn't believe them myself.

"O.K., then pull down your pants."

I obeyed.

Smack!

I clenched tighter. "That didn't even hurt!" The words dashed defiantly from some hidden corner of my soul never before revealed.

Smack! Smack!

The dam broke. I ran screaming through the backdoor.

* * *

The memory of that moment made my feet move. Buddy was on my heels, still trying to convince me to tarry 'til the three o'clock bell.

"C'mon, Sue Nell. You're no fun!"

I hesitated. I slowed further. The likely consequences chased each other, like headless chickens, around my own cerebral circuitry.

And then, with a sudden *Crack!,* my hesitation was broken by Jiminy's voice, "You must go to school."

I set off determinedly. To my surprise, Buddy followed.

We came around the corner and there it was: a red brick building with a white steeple. It had always been a place of fun for me; spring festivals, Little League games in the red Oklahoma dirt, an elephant slide in my classroom.

Now, it was the House of Dread.

And there *she* was, Miss Daisy, the school secretary. She had always been just like her name; a sweet smile, a helping hand, a pat on the head when I came seeking a band aid for my skinned knee.

But now, her chin—stiff. Her mouth—grim. Her eyes—narrowed. Someone had tipped her off.

I froze. Her eyes caught mine. I was trapped. Guilt and shame-ridden fear bit the back of my neck, clawed their way to my stomach, and turned my legs to pillars of salt.

Not Buddy's. He ran.

I looked at Miss Daisy. I swung my head around. I looked at Buddy. Looked at Miss Daisy. Buddy. Miss Daisy. Buddy. My moment of choice had come: to flee in the face of authority, to follow after Buddy whose backside receded defiantly through the flowerbed of a neighboring yard, to fly towards freedom...or to face the ones I feared.

Somewhere in that timeless moment, stretched by the "shoulds" and "shouldn't I's" of my inner debate, I saw the ears form on my friend as he trotted around the corner and out of sight.

I turned towards Miss Daisy. She was marching closer and closer. As her steps drew near, so did my dawn of adult understanding: the future with my captors held more freedom than Buddy's trail could ever promise.

I surrendered.

A PORTRAIT OF NANNY

Jack Sprat could eat no fat, his wife could eat no lean.
So between them both, you see,
They licked the platter clean.

Mother Goose

Kentucky has always been known for its gently rolling hills where Derby horses feed on the bluegrass and, where once a year, gentrified horsemen gather for the Great Race. In our family, it is also known as the birthplace of our "Pink Nanny."

Nanny, Nell Hooge Phillips, was my maternal grandmother. Besides Kentucky, she and the horses had one other thing in common—good breeding. The words of my mother often come back to me, "One thing you can always say about Nanny, she was well-bred. She was from a *very* aristocratic family."

Imagine...my Pink Nanny, soft and plump with rosy cheeks, just like a summer plum...an aristocrat!

On the wall, high up where there might be attic space in most houses, high up in my mother's bedroom with the cathedral ceilings, hung her other ancestral aristocrats. From two dark portraits, set in antique gold frames, stared great, great, great, great Uncle Samuel Carpenter, Jr., an attorney, and his father, The Honorable Samuel Carpenter, Sr., judge, both of Louisville, Kentucky. The father and son wore tall, starched collars, and black topcoats and ties beneath lofty cheekbones and hollowed faces. The short, cropped beard of Samuel Jr. made him a close likeness of Abraham Lincoln.

"Don't you think he looks distinctive?" my mother queried when she moved him from Nanny's attic to the bedroom gallery alongside his father.

***

Nanny stood four-feet eleven-inches tall and about four-feet around. The only time I remember seeing her high cheekbones was once after a particularly rigorous diet reinforced by diuretics given to her by a "quack" doctor. I have a photograph to remind me. Her usually soft, silvery hair is piled a bit stiffly on her head. Her rouge and powder accentuate those cheekbones while a thin belt accentuates her waist. Her early nineteen hundred's bust line, ample, is still in place. So is a floral print dress of lavender and blue. Nanny always did like violets.

No one knew how to diet quite like Nanny. She was always on one, but it was easy to forget, given her hundred and sixty-plus pounds and a recipe box full of Queen of Kentucky pudding, Mama's jam pie, and Grandma Elliot's fruit cake.

Right next to Uncle T. Ray, Jr.'s favorite, I recently came across this recipe:

Kentucky Burgoo—Toast of the Bluegrass State

800 lbs. soup meat	15 bushels Irish potatoes
4 dozen squirrels if in season	60 gallons canned tomatoes
24 gallons canned corn	6 gallons tomato puree
4 bushels onions	4 gallons canned carrots or
240 lbs. fat hens or roosters	2 bushels raw carrots
	200 lbs. cabbage

I remember one Sunday after church when we stopped by to invite Nanny out for lunch. She hesitated momentarily, then picked up her purse, "Well, I guess I can eat out since I've had my SEGO." (SEGO was the brand name of the latest liquid diet.) As long as she had consumed her SEGO, every other food item was on Nanny' hit list.

As an adult, whenever I visited my five-foot, one-inch, hundred and two-pound mother, and I was about to enjoy some peppermint ice cream, she would warn me, "You better watch out. You'll end up just like Nanny."

Both a threat and a promise.

Nanny's "good-breeding" surfaced in many of my mother's timely quotations. "Where's the party at?" one of us would yell. "Just before the 'at'," was the inevitable reply. My mother and Nanny were proud guardians of the King's English.

"Birds of a feather flock together," for those times when you brought home a friend of a "different background."

"Always wear clean underwear in case you're in an accident," which went well with, "Never wash your dirty linens in public." I don't know how the underwear always stayed clean, but I never saw any dirty linens in Nanny's house.

And my personal favorite, one that haunts me every time I am tempted to refer to my children as "kids": "If I'm a kid, you're a goat, and all the slop goes down your throat." Somehow the irony of someone named "Nanny" correcting with that quotation cannot escape me. But if we ever challenged Mother's proclamations, she quickly countered, "Who do you think taught *me* these things?"

Her mother, I supposed, but her mother was now my Pink Nanny.

Next to eating, the activity that Nanny enjoyed most in the world was talking. Actually, she probably enjoyed it more. She was the communication hub of the family. With three children, thirteen grandchildren, and several great-grandchildren before her death at age seventy-seven, she had plenty to keep her busy, and talking, and busy talking.

She also did her share of listening. Even with thirteen grandchildren, she managed to make each one feel they were the only one. When anyone went off to summer camp, they wrote to Nanny, and whenever anyone came home from college, Nanny was the first family member they went to see.

I remember one such visit by my brother Bill during Christmas of his freshman year of college in the late sixties. Nanny inquired, "Well, Bill, what do you plan to do with your education?"

He didn't hesitate, "I'm thinking about majoring in religion and running for God."

My eyes nearly popped out of my head waiting for her response to such a blasphemous remark. Unmoved and unprovoked, she calmly replied, "Now, I think that's funny, Bill, but don't you dare say that to your mother."

My poor mother. She spent endless hours on the phone when we were growing up. And it was always the same person on the other end of the line. Nanny called two to three times a day and talked for up to four hours. Whenever I came down the back hall and into the kitchen, Mother would be perched on the kitchen stool, phone clenched between her collarbone and ear, writing out a grocery list, peeling potatoes, or planning other tasks that she would most likely not complete that day. Sometimes she would leave the phone on the desk for a few minutes while she quickly *Cometed* the sink or blitzed the bathroom. Nanny never noticed Mother's absence and Mother had no trouble hearing Nanny's drone clear across the room.

In a desperate moment, Mother would motion for one of us to ring the back doorbell. Then she'd say, "Mother, I really hate to go, but there's someone at the door." After ten more minutes, she might be able to hang up.

If Nanny was not talking to Mother, she was talking to one of her "friends." The milkman, the laundryman, and the postman all thought she was so amusing, but I'm sure they had to add an extra thirty minutes to their routes on the days she managed to engage them. The laundryman of twenty years must have been her favorite—he made it into her will.

Speaking of which, Nanny's will was handwritten, and if it had not been a notarized document, you'd have thought she was still talking directly to you over coffee and pie.

"To Gordon Street [my father] I leave a thousand dollars for a horse because he always had time for me when nobody else did..."

"To Nell [my mother] I leave the dining room table, but I'm leaving the dining room chairs to Sue Nell because Nell never did like them anyway."

***

There were two parts to Nanny's house. They overlapped spatially, but in terms of time, they were past and present.

From the past, and by the front door, stood a stately mahogany secretary with a sterling silver letter opener. On the tables rested lead crystal paper weights with the busts of George Washington, Abraham Lincoln, and the recently assassinated John F. Kennedy. The bookcases held biographies of royalty and gentry, Mary Queen of Scots and Marie Antoinette among them.

By the side door rested a short and heavy sewing chest of indistinct ancestral background. In it waited a black, round tin of unmatched buttons and another tin for licorice and lemon drops. The licorice drops were for my dad. I always tried one and I always spit it out. The lemon drops were for me. Nanny filled the tin each time I came to spend the night, at least twice a month for twelve years.

When I spent the night at Nanny's, I slept in the double bed with plump, round finials in Nanny's room. Nanny slept beside me. Before we went to sleep I would pull her toes to help her arthritis.

When I woke up, Nanny was already busy in the kitchen. I would lie in bed, trying to follow the maze of blossoms linked by vines on the water-stained wallpaper. They reminded me more of strawberry runners with plump berries than flowers. Maybe that was because Nanny and Papa always fed me "Stwaberries!" for breakfast when I came to visit. They piled them high in a bowl around a mound of powdered sugar. The stems were left on so I could dip the strawberries in the sugar, then bite them off—all at once or a little at a time.

Also in Nanny's bedroom stood a large vanity with a tall, framed mirror. Handmade valentines decorated the frame, along with a letter or crayon drawing sent by a grandchild. Under the glass on the vanity top, Nanny kept yellowed excerpts from "Emily Post" or "Ann Landers." I found this one glued inside the lid to her recipe box:

"O God, give me the serenity to accept what cannot be changed, the courage to change what can be, and the wisdom to know one from the other."

Nanny was an Episcopalian. One of the drawers of her vanity guarded the veiled, velvety hats that she wore to church. Fortunately, the church was right across the street because Nanny never strayed too far or too often from her house. I never knew her to have a friend, outside of the deliverymen (though there are lots of recipes in her recipe box from a "Mrs. Kneeland"). I've often wondered why.

She did go to the grocery store. When she arrived home, she promptly checked off each and every item on the cash register tape to make sure she had not been mischarged. Nanny was far from miserly, but she was thorough and orderly. Maybe that's why she was Episcopalian.

When I got married, my mother gave me a copy of *Joy of Cooking* and a handwritten grocery list that Nanny had stuck inside Mother's copy when she married in 1939. The list included, among other things:

> matches—two boxes
> salt—Morton's
> French's mustard—one jar
> toilet paper, facial soap, and cleanser—two cans

She noted at the bottom, "I've given you a list of things necessary to start housekeeping. You should try to have $10 extra this first month for supplies as you are starting from scratch. Afterwards, $30 will be sufficient. Have as much fruit as possible for dessert." Advice she overlooked herself.

My parent's house burned down in 1980, and with it, the two portraits, high up on the wall. Gone are the great uncles, gone most of the family pictures. (A firefighter salvaged a few soggy prints and returned them after drying them on her living room floor.)

In his hallway, however, my brother Bill has a portrait of Nanny at about the age of twelve. The wooden oval frame encircles a little girl with bobbed hair and a bow larger than she. Striped tights disappear into black-laced leather shoes, on the bottom, and under a starched pinafore, on top. She is pretty and only slightly plump.

I have two pictures of Nanny. The one mentioned earlier with the high cheekbones in the blue and lavender dress. The other is soft, round, and powdery pink. I always have it with me. It's hung low in the hallway of my heart.

BOILED CUSTARD

Over the river and through the woods to Grandmother's house we go,
The horse knows the way to carry the sleigh through the ice and drifting snow-oh!

Jingle Bells

The splattered and stained recipe card reads "Boiled Custard." I can already imagine wrinkling noses and recoiling stomachs, but read on:

> 1 quart milk
> 6-8 mellow yellows of fresh eggs (the kind that stand to attention when fried)
> 2/3 cup sugar
> 1 tsp. vanilla

Bring the milk to just short of a boil, stirring continuously. Those seven minutes will crawl by, but you will be rewarded. Just before the film forms on the surface and the scorch on the underside, add the milk to the eggs, combined with 2/3 cup of sweetness, and return to the burner "until the mixture adheres to a wooden spoon." Remove from the heat. Cool. Again, take your time. Don't rush it.

But if you want, place the mixture in the fridge. When the heat has slipped away with the steam, add a teaspoon of vanilla bean ambar. Your nose will thank you, your tummy will thank you, and you will wonder how anything so simple, so pale, and so shapeless could be so sweet and good; like spring sunshine on the back porch.

***

This nectar is the legacy of Mary Erma Melinda McElhiney Street, born circa 1886 in Baxter Springs, Cherokee Kansas, just beyond the northern frontier of the Oklahoma Territory. Every afternoon in the 1950's and 60's, and perhaps for unwitnessed years before, she would place a glass of it on the otherwise bare nightstand of Granddaddy Street so that it would be the first thing he'd see, smell, taste, and savor when he awoke from his daily nap. A smack of his lips, and then "Ahhhh..."

On days of distraction or impatience, when the milk scorched or she removed the pot too soon, a glass of buttermilk would become the necessary substitute, but no one ever heard a smack and an "Ahhh..." inspired by a glass of buttermilk.

Occasionally, I would beg for a sample myself, but Grandmother was immoveable, steadfastly maintaining Granddaddy's rights to his boiled custard. It was the closest I ever saw her get to a demonstration of affection for her husband of more than fifty years.

For the most part, Grandmother's demeanor, along with her house, could be described as "staid." In the twenty plus years I visited Grandmother's house on 38th Street in Oklahoma City, it never changed, not even a misplaced chair or a vase of fresh flowers on the mahogany table in the living room. White linen tablecloths and napkins were exchanged due to the ebb and flow of gravy stains and spots left by homemade strawberry jam, but the rhythm of life was constant, measured by the ticking of the grandfather clock in the entry hall and embodied in the "still life" everywhere else.

There was some evidence, some "post-shadowing," of an earlier life. On the bookshelf near the front door, I found an ivory box, one-by-four inches long. The lid fit flush with the sides, concealing tiny tiles painted with dots and lines that lay orderly and patient inside. Outside, etched with the "red of fallen heroes" and the "green of the hope for independence," marched letters that I eventually realized spelled "MEXICO."

Once, in a picture album, I'd seen my brother Jimmy in a sombrero and chaps beside a plywood burro, somewhere south of the border with Grandmother and Granddaddy. The sepia colored photo reminded me of early movies where cowboys chased bandidos across the Rio Grande.

But that was it—no stories, tales, or explanations—leaving time and space for my own speculations. Regardless, I liked to spend the often long, quiet hours at Grandmother's stacking, matching dots, or lining up, like little soldiers, the miniature dominoes in their ivory tomb.

Alongside the dominoes was a leather shoe, cracked and brittle. It looked like it had once belonged to a toddling baby girl, but I couldn't be sure. I had seen pictures of my *dad* disguised in linen gowns up to age four. I had to wait patiently for the truth.

One day, whispering, Grandmother told me that it had belonged to Aunt Mary Louise.

Aunt Mary Louise was my dad's older sister. She had died at twenty-three of strep throat. It had gone straight to her heart within twenty-four hours, before the days of penicillin.

When he came home from the hospital without her, Granddaddy Street announced that he never wanted her name mentioned again. There was little talk of Uncle Bob Allen either, two years her junior, who was electrocuted a decade later while pumping out the basement during a spring storm.

I appreciated Grandmother breaking the rules, but I didn't have words to take away her pain.

As the only granddaughter after seven grandsons, I spent a night in the twin bed next to my grandmother's at least once a month. Before visiting, I changed my clothes. Grandmother did not like Levi's. She did not like play clothes, for that matter. If she happened to stop by unexpected, we could expect "the once over." Her eyes met ours, fell to our feet then slowly made their way back up to our faces. After a breathless pause, she'd begin, "If you're going with me..." and I'd already be half way to my room to find a pretty dress.

After the clothing change, I would apply a coat of Vaseline to my patent leather shoes, leaving a shine to rival any two matched limousines. Next, I'd remind myself to say "Yes, ma'am" and "Yes, sir."

"Did you go to Sunday School today?"

"Yeah."

"Yes, ma'am."

"Oh yeah. Yes, ma'am."

Although my mother was no slouch when it came to instructing us on the finer points of *Emily Post*, I learned most of my finer points of manners at Grandmother and Granddaddy Street's house. Granddaddy tried hard to reinforce the use of "Yes, sir" and "Yes, ma'am" with nickel bribes—but with negligible success. We did learn to stand when anyone older came into the room, and how to give "a firm handshake," essential during the thirty-six years of my grandfather's political career.

"Pick up from the left, serve from the right. Pick up from the left, serve..." No, that's not right. "Serve from the left, pick up from the right. Serve from the left...," essential fare when you're the designated hostess for the bridge ladies and pinochle men on Sunday evenings.

I practiced my skills at tea parties with crustless cucumber sandwiches, sugar cookies, and Grandmother's doll-sized cups and saucers at the coffee table. Later, I mastered them as I served ice water from the left and picked up empty glasses from the right in the dining room, Granddaddy flashing his famous grin above his equally famous and flashy bow tie.

From behind her cards at the bridge table, Grandmother hinted at her pride with a subtle smile. I would wait by her elbow, brow slightly lowered, yet not so much that my eyes couldn't peek out from under my neatly trimmed bangs.

"Oh, what a perfectly adorable little lady," Mrs. Adams would say, "And what nice manners!"

Score!

When my official duties had been fulfilled, I would excuse myself to the backyard. In Grandmother and Granddaddy Street's case, it was composed of the bare minimum: asphalt wide enough for Grandmother to back her yacht of a car out of the garage, handicapped by a sub-five-foot frame and "ample bosom." Both complicated her clearance of the boxwoods and garbage cans. Unadorned fescue grass, a clothesline beyond the eyes of curious neighbors, and a retaining wall, which kept the ferrous-tinted Oklahoma clay at bay during periodic thunderstorms punctuated by occasional tornadoes, abutted the asphalt.

I made a beeline to the retaining wall. Balanced on this six-inch cement beam, I paced and trekked to other worlds beyond good manners, teapots, and tiny cups painted with rose petals. Back and forth on my ten foot "Via Romana," I, Lisa Forrester, hiked over the Swiss Alps with my seven younger siblings, found passage across the Atlantic, and continued to protect and defend my charges in their new *patria*. All the while, I attended school where I got straight A's, of course, starred in the school musical, and excelled in dance, debate, and daring adventures of all kinds. (If this sounds vaguely familiar or transparently so, yes, I had seen "The Sound of Music" seven times between my seventh and eighth birthdays.)

During my travels, I resolved all manner of interpersonal conflict, delivered grand and wildly applauded speeches to a faceless, voiceless audience, and solidified my heroine status in a world where obstacles were too numerous to count—in stark contrast to my other life. No telling what the backyard neighbors thought as my monologues made their way through the red tips.

Thus I was able to manage the mostly solitary visits to Grandmother's, infinite hours interrupted only by the bass "doooongs" of the grandfather clock.

On days without bridge, Grandmother sewed, knitted, darned, canned peaches, and sang with an embarrassing "opera voice," the latter formerly esteemed as she made her way around the globe to entertain at International Rotary Club meetings. Now, however, it made everyone turn and stare when we sang "Oh God Our Help in Ages Past" from the balcony at Westminster Presbyterian Church.

I mention this litany of practical and performance skills because they are such rare phenomena in the extended Street family. No one else sews, at least not with any skill. (I can tell you all about the one dress, two pairs of overalls, three dress-shirts, and one-half nightgown that I made many years ago, but I doubt you would really care or be nearly as impressed as I was.)

Grandmother, on the other hand, had an entire room off the back hall just for her projects. When I was too old for them anymore, the smocked dresses she continued to make went to the Baptist Children's Home for orphans, several per week. Yet the room was always in perfect order; nary a stray thread or pile of gingham littered the counter or peeked out from a drawer. Even the sewing machine boasted its own custom-built home.

No one else in the family knits, beyond a scarf or two, but certainly not the pullovers for each grandchild with multiple colors and patterns, "knit one, pearl two," like those expensive Norwegian ones you see but never buy because they're just too much money.

And then there were the baby blankets--At age ninety, Grandmother crocheted the final one for my oldest son, Bryce. ("Just can't see well enough anymore," she apologized.) We still have the yellow postage-stamp of wool, reduced in size by half when my husband Jose threw it in the dryer. I cried because I knew there would be no more.

Each Christmas Eve, the Street family, including Cousins Wilda and Kate, gathered at Grandmother's house for dinner, presents, and Christmas carols. I never heard her play the grand piano at any other time of year, but after the last bow had been untied, and paper stuffed in boxes on the back porch, Grandmother would pull the music from the piano bench, spread "O, Little Town of Bethlehem" across the music stand, and call us to gather round. Despite the keys that wouldn't play, and the ones that played out of tune, we managed to maintain a pretty good pitch behind the strong vocals of Grandmother as we went "Over the River and Through the Woods," "Away in a Manger," and "Dashing Through the Snow." Something that had been silenced inside her seemed to find its way out on that one holy night.

Taking her lead from Granddaddy, named "the most economical man in the 13th legislature" by then Oklahoma Governor Murray, Grandmother could be called, with complete objectivity, frugal. There were a few befuddling exceptions.

She drove a Lincoln Continental, with buttons to change gears, as she chauffeured Granddaddy around town. On cold winter evenings, she wore a mink stole to the gala events required of public figures. And, her right ring finger hosted a two-karat diamond. (The latter could be attributed to

Granddaddy as well, who claimed to have accepted it in exchange for a funeral during the Depression when diamonds were evidently more plentiful than dollars.)

In contrast, she saved and reused aluminum foil off the backs of baked potatoes, and she minced both her words and her Benjamins.

One year in early December, she asked my mother, "What would Sue Nell like for Christmas?"

Careful to be conservative with her suggestion, Mother offered, "How about I pick up a nightgown for her and you can sign the card?"

"That would be fine. How much do you think it will be?"

"Oh, I'd say around seven dollars," mother estimated.

When the receipt for nine dollars was turned over the next day, Grandmother exchanged it for a pre-written check followed by, "You said seven dollars."

One day in 1965, nine years into my orderly, restrained relationship with my grandmother, it changed forever. I changed forever.

She called and invited me to the movies. I had gone to the occasional Disney film at the Lakeside Theater on May Avenue with a friend or sibling and, of course, to the Tower seven times to see Maria and the Von Trapp children, but never to a movie with a parental or grandparental figure. Mother and Daddy never went to movies. Once we tried one at a drive-in, but when I complained that there was too much hugging and kissing, in other words, sex, my mother agreed and we left.

This was different. This was a mid-day outing with my grandmother, who didn't do outings with her grandchildren, at least not in my lifetime.

The movie was *Shenandoah* starring Jimmy Stewart and the "ruggedly handsome" Doug McClure. A review in the *New York Times* described it as a "four hanky...dramatic allegory underscoring the futility of war" and featuring, among many other controversial moments, the "reunion of a young white and black soldier" in a Virginia field. This was a Saturday in Oklahoma in 1965, in a state settled by many from the confederate south who had still not forgotten their roots, a state where unbridled and noble post-World War II patriotism flew from every corner and doorpost.

I cried my way through the entire one hundred and five minutes and clearly remember stepping out of midnight darkness in the theater to the blinding brightness of mid-afternoon—holding my grandmother's hand. My eyes and heart and mind were not the same as the ones I had awakened with that morning; innocence lost, darkness revealed, somewhere in the middle of a Civil War battlefield.

There, sons and fathers had perished suddenly and with savagery, or drop by drop as their lives seeped slowly into a recently plowed meadow...somewhere in the middle of a Civil War battlefield where friends murdered, sometimes each other, or embraced one long held at arm's length.

I came out holding the hand of my grandmother who perhaps had new eyes too, and saw me, saw my broken heart and opened mind, and wept with me. Sweetness and goodness in the afternoon sun.

-6-

COUSIN WILDA

Still waters run deep.

Only once did I go with Daddy to pick up Cousin Wilda before our annual Christmas Eve dinner at Grandmother and Granddaddy Street's. She lived in a dark den of an apartment all by herself and had worked hidden away in a back office of the county clerk for twenty-seven years. Yet, out she came each December, trailing the tinsel and accompanied by cranberry sorbet.

I'd seen a picture of her somewhere, standing outside a buff-brick, three-story building with black iron bars on the windows. She was squinting in the bright sun and I know why. The inside of her basement apartment had no light—well, almost no light. The bulbs were perhaps forty watt and layered with dust so thick that the inside had no more than the amber glow of a windowless bar. I felt kind of ashamed...of me or her, I'm not sure.

Wilda Addell McElhiney was the only surviving child of Grandmother Street's oldest brother, long deceased, William Akers McElhiney. An infant brother had died, and the only reason Wilda hadn't joined him was due perhaps to the desperate attempts of her parents, and the fierce, stubborn, even a bit angry determination of Wilda herself. She outlived seventeen operations and almost all her blood relatives.

In my mind's eye, Wilda seemed shriveled—like perhaps she'd once been bigger, but life had sucked all the height and plumpness right out of her. She was no more than four foot ten. Not even heels could add a smidgen to her height—no one sold them in size two.

When I went shoe-shopping with my mother, she would often pick up an extra pair in the children's department for Wilda. Meaning, of course, that Wilda often wore the same Mary Jane's or shiny patent leathers with a bow across the toe that I did.

I liked Wilda. She talked a little funny and had a scar that split her upper lip, but she would always sit and chat with me between the pumpkin pies and "The First Noel" on Grandmother's grand piano.

And when it came time for unwrapping gifts, I looked forward to Wilda's more than any other. Every year she gave me a Madame Alexander doll—one from India, another from Scotland, even three of the four "Little Women," Beth, Jo, and Meg. I suspect my mother picked them up for her because Wilda never went anywhere beyond work and the grocery store. Even then, she'd complain that pig-tailed little girls would whisper and stare and giggle with a hand over their mouths, as if she couldn't see. I never giggled. Wilda was my very best first-cousin-once-removed.

When Granddaddy Street moved from "this life to more life," as my pastor likes to say, Wilda moved from the basement to Granddaddy's bedroom.

"She's getting kind of old," Grandmother explained, at nine years her senior.

Wilda and Grandmother bickered a bit, as old women are inclined to do, but for the most part they got along quite nicely, especially with the extra three hundred dollars that Grandmother collected each month for Wilda's room and board.

Shortly after Wilda moved in, Daddy decided to move seven hundred miles away to the mountains of Colorado and near the cabin that his mother had built back in the twenties. Wilda just couldn't believe that he'd go off and leave his mother all alone after fifty-two years, but he promised to return often.

Every three or four months, he made the commute back home to the humidity of Oklahoma to look after their affairs. Once he tried to convince Wilda to move her savings from a passbook account, earning one or two percent, to a more lucrative Certificate of Deposit, but she refused to mess with such a thing. It was just too complicated. She named him her heir anyway, despite his meddling, seeing as there was no one else alive with her blood in their veins and the vigor of sub-golden years.

At sixty-five, Daddy died. Wilda was eighty-four and Grandmother, ninety-three. It just didn't seem fair at all. Despite a stroke a few months later, Grandmother hung on determinedly, her devotion to Wilda and duty to her brother sustaining her, despite being "good for nothing."

Three years later, a frail, sickly, almost-alone-Wilda finally passed at eighty-seven, Grandmother following in three months. Knowing my grandmother would not be far behind her, I didn't make the cross-country trek to Wilda's funeral, but Lord knows she merited the honor.

When her will was read, my mother dismissed the raised eyebrows of Aunt Betty, who had also married into the family, when it was discovered that Wilda had left everything to "Nell Phillips Street."

"Oh, don't worry," Mother assured her, "She couldn't have much of anything anyway."

Her checkbook proved otherwise: line after line, year after year, check after check; one for ten dollars, another for twenty-five, occasionally a fifty, all written to the American Cancer Society, the Shriner's Hospital for Crippled Children, the March of Dimes. Many other children around the world who talked funny with a split upper lip would get what she never had: a life without ridicule, a life without shame, a life lived in the light. And my mother got the remaining hundred thousand.

NANNY'S HOUSE

By the light, of the silvery moon,
I want to spoon,
To my honey I'll croon love's tune.
Honey moon, keep a-shinin' in June.
Your silv'ry beams will bring love's dreams,
We'll be cuddlin' soon,
By the silvery moon.

Edward Madden as sung on *Sing Along with Mitch*

A while back, I got an email from Cousin Janie Phillips. For over a year she'd been urging me to return to Oklahoma City, land of red dirt, the Ole Cimarron, and my ancestral roots, "to see how much it's changed," she said. (I understood for the better.) It had been sixteen years since my mother's funeral, our final Phillips reunion on Oklahoma soil.

I must say, that reunion left me with many warm memories. It was a week after the Oklahoma City bombing, and Oklahomans, in the face of immense tragedy, were at their finest. Thousands of volunteers poured in, southern hospitality rose to new heights. Sandwiches were made, beds provided, hands held, and along church halls, in streets, and over the airwaves, floated amazing grace. We, the Street-Phillips clan, arrived from all over the country, accompanied by fresh firefighters who continued the search for survivors.

While awash in shock and grief, I felt proud to be an Oklahoman. With my children in tow, we visited the mournful site of the bombing where thousands had left teddy bears, candles, and poems. We also visited the site of my birth. We toured the streets where I had ridden my Schwinn to Nichols Hills Elementary, the park where I played hooky in kindergarten, and the Country Club pool where I impressed (stunned) my friends and myself with a one-and-a-quarter flip off the high dive. My children, who have grown up in more modest environs, stared wide-eyed and open-mouthed at the seven chimneys, tennis courts, and circular drives of some the more recent additions to the "hood."

But back to Cousin Janie's email.

"Things in Nichols Hills are really changing," she wrote. "They've knocked down all the homes between Huntington and Windsor to make room for new, super-sized ones. You remember, that's where Mrs. Rainey's used to be."

Mrs. Rainey was Mother's best friend in Oklahoma City and her home was one to which many of us might aspire: a red brick colonial with floors and interior wood trim polished by years of lemon oil and children's feet, hands, and bottoms as they slid down the stairs or railing...in many towns and cities across the country, a home to be protected and defended for its historical character and contributions.

And then Janie added the words that pierced my heart: "I saw Nanny's [our grandmother's] house up on a trailer the other day—at least they're moving it somewhere and not tearing it down."

Since Nanny's death, it's been impossible to imagine other little feet running down her hallway, occasionally blistering toes on the metal floor-grate of early central heating, or strangers' fingers picking strawberries beyond the backyard fence. But to think that they have taken her home away and I know not where it's laid—unthinkable.

Nanny, my maternal grandmother, was immortalized in another of my stories, yet her house deserves a tender, thoughtful eulogy as well.

It was quite small by Nichols Hills' standards, but then it wasn't quite in Nichols Hills. Her two-bedroom, one-bath rambler with a single-car garage sat facing Pennsylvania Avenue, a major northwest Oklahoma City artery, across from All Souls Episcopal Church. The street was so busy I was never allowed to cross. I had to content myself with the front steps and Nanny's voice drifting through the open door from the kitchen table, or as a silent observer alongside Papa in his workshop.

The modest exterior was perfectly Nanny in my child's mind. She and Papa had painted its bricks white in my earliest years. An interminably long and narrow driveway, with wandering cracks, approached the front steps, the grass edged and trimmed carefully each week by Papa's shears.

Later, Nanny had the bricks sand-blasted, revealing the red clay beneath, yet leaving behind bits of white paint. The effect was almost pink, matching the cheeks of my "Pink Nanny." (I think the sand-blasting might have been my mother's idea since I don't remember Nanny and Papa ever doing anything else to alter or update the aesthetics of their home. Their retirement income from many years of insurance sales didn't allow it, or perhaps they had arrived at a time and an attitude where the comfort of the familiar was more important than new decor.)

Nanny's house had three doors. Those who entered through the front were door-to-door salespeople: the Fuller Brush man, the Hoover vacuum vendor, and the Avon lady. Or they were someone coming for a more formal visit: grandchildren home from college, a mourner after Papa's funeral. These folks entered the "parlor" where two winged-back chairs framed a velveteen loveseat. Facing the threesome, a fireplace graced the room...but never hosted a fire. The mantle displayed Papa's pipes, with his canes close at hand, and a tall cherry wood secretary rose to the right of the door. I believe it now casts a watchful eye in the home of my cousin Sue. (Or is it at Sally's?)

There must have been a table because Nanny proudly displayed her collection of crystal paperweights etched with famous presidents—one of whom was "Old Rough and Ready" Zachary Taylor. He was famous (or infamous) as a hero of the Mexican-American war and, while an owner of a hundred slaves, a strident opponent to slave-state expansion. After marrying Nanny's distant cousin, he became the short-lived (sixteen months), twelfth president of the United States.

At the far end of the parlor, a cherry wood table, accompanied by eight caned Queen Anne chairs, mourned its solitude until the next holiday dinner. As far as I know, the table and chairs never celebrated another until they traveled many miles to *my* house, which might explain why the caning survived Nanny's generation. It failed with my children's pre-adolescent knees and Nikes, and had to be replaced with hard seats and upholstery. (An error in judgment on my part; plastic would have better withstood the mashed peas and potatoes.)

In any case, Nanny's front door and the parlor, although occasionally used, did not enter her home or her heart. For that you had to go through the back door.

The back door served as entrance for the mailman, the laundryman (as in he who picked up shirts and pants to be laundered and starched), the milkman (yes, we all had delivery of glass-bottled whole milk and cartons of cottage cheese in those days), and Nanny's thirteen grandchildren. It opened to the den with its brick-look linoleum, T.V., sofa, and a third door that led "out back" to the flower garden, Papa's shop, and the mostly uncultivated yard beyond the fence where Papa grew a few vegetables and strawberries. To be perfectly honest, like the parlor, the den wasn't used much either, except as a place for Nanny to stand (or sit) and talk, and for all three of us to sing along with Mitch.

But by the back door rested a particularly important piece of my childhood and one that, despite its diminutive size (yet enormous weight) has survived moves from Oklahoma City, to Colorado, to Seattle, to Wisconsin, to Portland, to Atlanta, to western Oregon, and finally to Bend on the east side of the Cascades, where we currently reside.

Nanny's sewing chest.

Her sewing chest reminds me of Nanny: short and stout. But there they diverge. The chest has an unassuming, humble nature. Nanny, on the other hand, assumed much and was quite proud. While now retired at the entrance to our hallway beneath a collection of cracked and leathered books, over its lifetime the sewing chest has held a variety of treasures. At least until my departure from Oklahoma City at age twelve, it housed three very important items.

First, a button box—yes, the same button box into which I now throw the spares that come with a new blouse or sweater, or where I drop a random fastener found on the floor whose origins I cannot trace. I still recognize many a pearl or brass button that I sorted and sized and patterned and shaped when I was a young child on an overnight visit. The mundane morphed into castles and daisies and approving friends' smiling faces. Meanwhile, Nanny cooked and talked (or talked and cooked), and Papa trimmed.

Next to the button box and above the drawer that still houses navy, beige, and red spools of thread—plus the chartreuse, lavender, and ochre of long ago recycled fashions— sat two additional tins. The first held black licorice drops, quite nasty to my five-year-old taste buds. They were reserved not for me, or any of my twelve siblings and cousins who shared my opinion, but for my dad, Gordon, to whom Nanny also left a thousand dollars so he could "buy the horse he always wanted." (By the time he received the money for the horse, I guess he'd grown beyond wanting one...but he never outgrew his love for licorice.)

The second tin held lemon drops!—hard candies about the size and shape of a thimble, their bright yellow dimmed by a dusting of baker's sugar. They were sweet, not the puckery kind I grew to love when I got older, and I adored them. Even now, my eyes grow large and my mouth gets all watery just remembering.

I arrived for a sleep-over with Nanny and Papa a couple times a month, and I was never disappointed—the lemon drops were waiting. As far as I ever knew, they were just for me. I'd venture to guess that each one of us thirteen grandchildren believed the same thing.

Yet, Nanny's house nurtured many other memories as well. Its true center was around the kitchen table. Nanny was almost always there. If she wasn't cross-checking the accuracy of her grocery bill with the boxes of recently delivered goods, she was re-telling stories, interviewing (interrogating) us about our latest life events, and preparing a chicken pot pie for the oven.

One evening, just before Christmas (I remember because I was headed for a hayrack ride at the stables where I was taking English riding lessons), I sat in front of that same oven, its door lowered to welcome a batch of tea cookies or perhaps to take the chill off the evening air. I began rocking back and forth on Nanny's words and the rear legs of one of her kitchen chairs, more occupied with her tale than caution. Suddenly, I flipped over backwards, my leg went into the oven, and my right knee sizzled on the pre-heated rack—a rather unusual accident, to say the least.

Nanny raced, as best she could on her four-foot, eleven-inch, hundred-and-sixty-pound frame, to the medicine cabinet, grabbed some "salve," whatever that was, slathered it on my knee, applied some ice, and then wrapped it with gauze and a pretty spectacular looking bandage. Mother, Nan, was there too, and her contribution, befitting her concern for aesthetics, was to place a sticker, the kind you had to lick, across the top of the bandage. Beneath a sprig of holly, it wished a bright, "Merry Christmas!" I was ready for the party.

The back of Nanny's house, the part visited only by family or those needing to use the bathroom, was accessed by a long, creaky hallway covered by an incredibly thin carpet that had been manufactured at least seventy-five years earlier. Beyond the aforementioned grate, through which escaped groaning sounds as the heat kicked into high gear, there was a built-in medicine cabinet. That's where Nanny kept, among other things: salve, Ivory soap (it truly does float—or did) cod liver oil, and Vick's VapoRub.

Recently, a nighttime cough wracked my body. The Vick's called to me from its hiding place in the bottom of a bathroom drawer, and when I unleashed its intense menthol vapors, memories of Nanny rubbing it on my congested chest filled my mind and room. I dabbed a bit on my chest...then had second thoughts. I remembered using it a few years ago to kill a vicious fungus that had taken over my big toe and nail. The nail eventually dissolved and fell off—twice—taking the fungus with it. I felt a bit of alarm at what Vicks might be doing this time as it began to burn. Oh well, it worked for Nanny, I guessed it would work for me. I slept like a baby.

Speaking of sleep, by the time I took the stage, my parents had it made. If my four brothers weren't available to babysit, I had Nanny and Papa to welcome me into their arms and beds. Occasionally I slept in the other twin in Papa's room, but mostly I remember high jumping myself onto Nanny's four-poster double, meters above the hardwood floor, and snuggling up next to her.

Before long she would ask, "Could you pull my toes?"

O.K., at this rather odd request, most adults would recoil with the same distaste reserved for raw calves' liver, but evidently it helped relieve her arthritis. Any adoring grandchild, too young for adult prejudices, would have equally acquiesced.

In her bedroom, Nanny also had a dressing table. It was crowned by a mirror decorated with recent and yellowed Valentine cards formed by misshapen hearts, many scrawled with, "I love you, Pink Nanny." I can still see both her pile of silver curls and me, perched on a nearby stool, reflected in the mirror. Almost always she'd let me take the shine off my nose with her powder puff, also pink. It waited in a round, cut-glass dish, capped with sterling silver, right next to her rouge. *Where are they now?*

Nanny's house. Where is *it* now? Is anyone standing on the back steps listening, late for their next delivery? Or sitting on them, like my brother Tommy, eating balls of white bread rolled by tiny fingers, Nanny's story-telling continuing non-stop from behind the screen door? Are there little feet running down the hallway? Are there more toes to pull or strawberries to taste?

Nanny's house. Where is it now?

Tucked under a featherbed of memories where no trailer can haul it away.

MY LULA

Jesus loves me, this I know,
For the Bible tells me so.
Little ones to Him belong,
They are weak, but He is strong...

She had strong arms and hands. They were almost magical. She could balance me on her hip, hum or sing one of her Jesus songs, and slice, boil, and whip potatoes for the gravy and "Lula's fried chicken," all at the same time without stopping to ask someone else to take a turn cuz her arm was givin' out.

Almost like an extra arm or leg, I followed her around the kitchen, rollin' out cherry pie dough, answerin' phone calls, "Street's residence!," sweepin' up flour, sugar, and little pieces of crust, and tastin' the brownies before and after they went into the oven. I was her "Bright Eyes, shinin' in the dark," and she was "My Lula."

Lula wore a white, crisp uniform with matching nurse's shoes when she arrived each morning—Monday, Wednesday, and Friday—until she left just before dusk.

"Gotta get home before dark," she'd say, "Lot's of baaaaad people out there these days."

When all the chairs at the dining room table were filled, with the addition of Jack and Jimmy home from college, she'd come five days a week and stay through dinner. The only exception was her annual vacation in the spring. Every year it was the same: she went to Mississippi with the other ladies from her church for a "revival." Lula was the only person I knew who went to revivals, so I assumed it was something only colored folks did.

"So are you going to Mississippi in April, Lula?" Daddy would ask.

"I sure am, Mr. Street. Ev'ry year. And I'm praying the Lord will give me a new car, cuz I sure does need a new car."

Mother and Daddy smiled with one of their, "Isn't that nice, but it's never gonna happen" type smiles. Mother had told me that Lula made twenty-seven dollars a week, nine dollars a day. She was appalled that other neighbors were paying fifty a week to their girls who weren't anywhere near as good of workers as Lula, "like throwing money out the window." *How on earth could Lula pray or pay for a new car?*

Sure enough, a few weeks before the annual pilgrimage, Lula pulled up at eight o'clock in the morning in a brand spankin' new, cherry red Chevy Malibu.

"Where'd ya get that, Lula?" Daddy asked, with disbelieving eyes.

"Well, Mr. Street, I told you the Lord was gonna get me a new car and He surely did."

Lula did a lot for my early faith formation.

Lula was Baptist. We were Presbyterian. She didn't smoke, drink, play cards, or dance. She underlined words in her Bible every day in red ink, and she was never not singin' or hummin' one of her "Praise Jesus" songs that I'm sure never found their way into any hymnals. (All of the above would have disqualified her from being a good Presbyterian.)

Lula also made a great "Preacher Pie." Now, the funny thing about Preacher Pie was its secret ingredient: a good dose of premium Kentucky bourbon. Lula would make it for us at Thanksgiving, Christmas, or other special occasions, and before cutting the first slice, eyes closed in a moment of holy reverence, Daddy'd call down a blessing from heaven, and pronounce, "Lula, you sure do make a good Preacher Pie!"

"Why *preacher* pie?" you might ask. Preacher Pie got its name from the every Sunday afternoon visits of Lula's preacher. Each week, after the morning service and before the evening one, he would show up at her door, hat in hand, belt slightly loosened, and sit down for an extra big piece with an extra big smile. He was never the worse for it, and never admitted knowing the secret ingredient. As he tipped his hat on the way back to the pews, I suspect he also exclaimed, "Lula, you surely do make a good Preacher Pie!"

***

Lula lived in Jones, Oklahoma. Jones was east of Nichols Hills where we lived. It was east of Western Avenue. It was beyond Westminster and over the railroad tracks. As far as I knew, only colored people lived in Jones on the other side of the tracks.

Jones was out in "the country," out where there was no running water, although Lula had one of those really neat hand pumps in her yard. Lula's house had no central heating, maybe no heating at all, and she certainly didn't have indoor plumbing.

One day I got up my nerve to ask the question that was itchin' my insides. "Where do you...go?" I said.

"Oh, I have me a proper outhouse, Bright Eyes," Lula was quick to reply.

Now I was familiar with outhouses, havin' gone to the Colorado mountains every summer of my life and havin' once spent three hours in an outhouse with seven people. Ellen Records got to sit on the throne during a torrential rainstorm punctuated by hail at Coney Creek. We'd ridden there under clear skies one morning to pull in a rainbow trout or two. While it poured, we sang, "I've Been Workin' on the Railroad," "Silvery Moon," and every other campfire song we could think of. So I *knew* outhouses.

But Lula's answer didn't quite satisfy my itch. "What do you do at night?" I asked.

"Well, I have me a chamber pot under the bed."

I was still too young to have read any Victorian novels that featured hand-painted, porcelain chamber pots for nightly needs, so I was stumped. What was a chamber pot? I had to find out.

Besides, Lula raised chickens. Daddy and his grandmother McElhiney had raised chickens. He loved to tell me how he'd put a few in her bed to give her a good scare from time to time, back when he was my age, and he couldn't stop chucklin' fifty years after his grandma's last scream—all of which left me with a great fondness for the idea of chicken cultivation.

Thus, I began a campaign to get Mother to let me go visit Lula at her house with the chickens and the chamber pot in Jones, Oklahoma, across Western Avenue, and on the other side of the tracks.

Now this may seem like an innocent enough outing, but let me remind you that this was Oklahoma in the early sixties when colored people still "knew their place." Even years later, Mrs. Truman, the most widely read and quick-witted woman I knew in the City, told me of a time when her maid was on loan to my recently widowed mother. The telephone rang one afternoon, and Elinor answered, "Nell Street's residence."

"I blew...my...top when I heard about it!" Mrs. T said. "Elinor was just being uppity." Her indignant tone left no room for a more favorable interpretation.

I scratched my head. "What *should* she have said?" I asked.

"Why, 'the Gordon Street residence,' of course."

Of course: in honor of my deceased father.

In 1961, there was certainly never any socializing between blacks and whites in Oklahoma. We were never allowed to go to Spring Lake amusement park anymore "after the negroes took over." I missed the "Big Dipper" roller coaster a lot. There were no black children in my school. Heck, there was only one Catholic! Granted, there were a number of Jews.

Tommy Shanker was one of them. One day in sixth grade he came to school, nostrils flaring like a bull ready to charge. With righteous indignation, he took me to account.

"My family was not allowed to join the Country Club, "*your* Country Club," he said, "because we are Jewish."

I couldn't believe it. I had just finished reading *The Diary of Anne Frank* and was feeling rather sympathetic towards Jews. I carried his indignation home with me and confronted my parents, crossing my fingers that his accusation wasn't true.

"Tommy Shanker told me that his family can't join the Country Club because they're Jewish. Is that true?"

Awkwardly, even a little sheepishly, my father admitted it was.

"But what about the Schonwalds? They're Jewish. They're members!"

"Well—they're different." (The Schonwald's son was my cousin Kent's best friend and the duo had recently played golf with my brother Bill. This seemed to be O.K. because there was no chance that Bill would marry him.)

Seeing that Daddy was having some misgivings about this ambivalent state of social standards, my mother jumped in to clear up any confusion left by his troubled conscience.

"Well, you know, when Jews get involved in things, they have a tendency to take over," she said.

Really? I had no idea. I thought of my friends Leslie and Linda, Kip, and Tommy. I wasn't convinced. I marched off with a nascent sense of injustice rising in my bosom.

***

But back to Lula's house. I hatched a plan. I decided to celebrate my next birthday with a trip to Lula's "farm." I would invite a few of my best friends: Bobby Eskridge, Kathy Upsher, Laurie MacIvor, and the likes, and we would chase chickens, eat them fresh and fried on Lula's iron stove, and help roll out homemade biscuits to be relished with hand-churned butter, clover honey, and flour all over our fingers and faces.

I proposed the idea to Mother. I'm sure she was more than a bit hesitant, but after serious begging and pleading on my part, she somehow gave in.

"Oh well, it will be a grand adventure!" she admitted, "and no one will look after you better than Lula."

Before long, all the arrangements were made. Thinking back on it now, I can't believe that the other mothers agreed to let their five year olds go out to their neighbor's maid's house for a picnic with the chickens in Jones, Oklahoma, on the other side of the tracks. But they did.

It was wonderful. Lula's house was all dressed up for the occasion; when we peeked in the bedroom, a bright orange satin bedspread with fringe dazzled our eyes. Plates from Niagara Falls, Kansas City, the Lincoln Memorial, and the Golden Gate Bridge, gifts from my parents NSM travels (National Something Mortician meetings—I never knew what the "S" stood for) circled the living room on a custom-built shelf. Hundreds of sets of salt and pepper shakers—baby ducks, a boy and girl leaning in for a kiss, toadstools and dairy cows—crowded every horizontal surface. It was amazing and mesmerizing to our five-year-old eyes. We'd never seen anything like it in our *Architectural Digest* homes.

And it was only the beginning. Soon we were chasing Herman and Daisy around the yard, feathers flying, trying out the outhouse and water pump, and oooing and ahhhing over Lula's tasty fryers. Did I mention it was wonderful?

But even better, when my friends returned home at the end of the day, I got to spend the night in Lula's bed under the orange satin bedspread. She slept on a cot in the living room and I have to admit, I was a bit jealous. (If I had stayed

another night, I'd have asked her to swap me out.) Last, but
not least, I got to use the speckled pot under the bed in the
wee hours for my nightly needs.

***

In the summer, we went for a month to Allenspark in the
mountains of Colorado. There were seven of us, two
keeshonds, and Lula in a Mercury station wagon with no air
conditioning.

The best trip was when Grandmother Street sent us off with
a box full of eight tiny presents, one to open in each town
along the perfectly flat, breathless, sultry highway that ran
through Watonga, Kingfisher (where Daddy got stopped every
year by the local speed trap—a tradition we would have been
disappointed to miss), Woodward, Boy's (Boise) City (where my
four brothers delighted in yelling, "Get down, Sue Nell! They
arrest little girls and throw them in jail here!"), Guymon,
Lamar, Limon, and finally Longmont. We paused long enough
to buy a month's worth of groceries, and then, back bumper
dragging on the roadway, left the valley behind to head up the
South St. Vrain River to "God's Country" and "The Old Cabin."

The worst trip perhaps was when Bill threw up all over
Jack's face while he was sleeping and Daddy wouldn't stop but

told Mother to clean it up with lemonade. (Could this really be true? That's the story I've been told and I'm stickin' by it.)

But my strongest memory of our Oklahoma City-Allenspark treks was a lunch stop in the Oklahoma panhandle when I was about eight or nine. We pulled into a local Woodward diner, Lula pulled out her brown bag lunch, and the rest of us headed in for a treat of air conditioning, club sandwiches, and root beer floats.

As we sat in the booth scanning the menu, bare legs avoiding the cracks in the vinyl seats, a lady-looking-in-charge came up to our table.

"Excuse me," she interrupted, "I noticed you have a colored woman sitting in your car."

We couldn't imagine where she was going with this.

"Yes, she's our maid," Daddy explained.

"Well, at our church, we believe that if you cut a colored person's finger and you cut a white person's finger, they both bleed red, so we would be happy to have her come in and eat with you in our restaurant."

Her logic seemed pretty sound, but I have to admit, I had never considered such a thing. This was just the way it was. Tommy, Bill, and I all sat hushed and wide-eyed on the edge of our seats. There was no quick response.

***

My thoughts flashed to the time when we were on the Lincoln Turnpike between Oklahoma City and Tulsa, and I almost didn't get my green pistachio ice cream in Howard Johnson's best ever, "over-the-freeway" diner. It was the highlight of every trip we made to northeast part of the state.

But once, when we entered the restaurant, we took an extra long time getting seated. While I waited for the hostess to give me crayons and a page out of a coloring book, I became aware of a whispered conversation between Mother and Daddy. Mother signaled the counter with a glance and a nod, and I looked that direction as well. Four people dressed in their "Sunday-go-to-meetin'-clothes" were seated there with their menus open, waiting to order. I leaned in closer to hear my parents' words.

After a minute or so of eavesdropping, I realized Mother and Daddy were discussing whether we should sit down at one of the empty booths or not. It had something to do with the people at the counter. Suddenly, it dawned on me that I might not get my grilled-cheese sandwich and pistachio ice cream with the clown face.

"Why can't we just sit over there next to the window?" I asked.

Mother's eyes widened a bit more, her lips pursed, her jaw tightened.

"I guess that would be all right, wouldn't it, Babe?" Daddy said, as boldly as he dared.

"C'mon," I pleaded. "This is the only place you can get *green* ice cream in an over-the-freeway diner…and you promised we could!"

After a few more hushed exchanges, I was cheerfully sliding around the circular vinyl benches in the corner, as far from the people at the counter as possible.

***

A burst from the air conditioner brought me back to Woodward. Clearly Daddy was as confused and taken back as we were.

"Well, actually… she's more comfortable out there," he finally offered.

The restaurant owner tried again, "Really, we'd be glad to have her come inside."

"No, really, it's O.K. She prefers to be in the car," Mother said.

We gazed out the window. Lula sat chewing her PB and J, watching the heat roll off the blacktop in watery waves.

Perhaps she would never know what we knew: she was more comfortable in the hundred degrees, hundred percent humidity of a western Oklahoma July, with two panting dogs and a sack lunch in the back of a station wagon, than she could ever be having a grilled-cheese sandwich and chocolate shake in a Woodward diner, surrounded by those she had loved so long and so well.

My Lula.

THAT'S WHAT IT'S ALL ABOUT

You put your right foot in,
You put your right foot out,
You put your right foot in and you shake it all about,
You do the Hokey Pokey and you turn yourself around,
That's what it's all about!

Kindergarten dance
Nichols Hills Elementary Spring Festival

Just beyond the chain-linked fence, I could see a quilt of patchwork families spread out on blankets all over the ball fields. They encircled the swing sets, toasted their neighbors with lemonades and sweetened iced teas, called to a toddler who was making her way up the slide, and strained necks to catch a glimpse of us—of me.

I smelled recently fried chicken (not the kind from KFC, but from the iron skillets and skilled hands of stay-at-home mothers—or their maids), along with baked beans sweetened with molasses and what was left of the Betty Crocker "extra-moist" brownies after we'd helped our mothers clean the bowls earlier in the day.

I could feel the energy in the air, in our feet, and in our chests as our hearts doubled their beat in anticipation of our grand entrance. But I couldn't hear anything. The blood had rushed into my ears and blocked all sound save my own trembling voice that both cheered and choked me with anticipation and doubt. *What if I trip? What if I hop, but forget to step? What if I mix up my left and right?*

And then there was the issue of Kip. Kip Hilstein was my partner. We already had our hands crossed—under-over, right over left—except I had to let go to wipe off the sticky sweat from his limp limbs from time to time. And I already knew that he wouldn't be able to step-hop—or that if he did, it wouldn't be at the same time as my own—and that he might add in an extra hop for good measure, but it wouldn't be good at all.

I only had myself to blame. Miss Apostle had assigned me to Becky Flint who could skip just fine. There were more girls than boys in our kindergarten class, and not everyone could have a boy. Somehow, I already knew a boy was the better deal and I wanted one. Somehow, I didn't figure Kip counted.

At five, Kip already marched, danced, and skipped to a different drummer. At five, it was already clear to everyone that Kip was a genius, arriving everyday with a new "invention" of his to share during "Show and Tell," always playing with the tinker toys and Lincoln Logs, the erector set and the miniature microscope. I'm sure he asked for one of those chemistry sets in a wooden box for Christmas—except that he was Jewish— but I bet he got one for Hanukkah.

But being a genius didn't make him a "catch," even in kindergarten, so somehow I felt Miss Apostle had had the last laugh. Kip and I stood poised, as the shortest in the class, to be the first out on the blacktop with our step-hop-hop at the 1962 Spring Festival.

Suddenly, my ears cleared and I heard the music that had accompanied thousands of skippers before me as they prepared to entertain moms, dads, brothers, sisters, grandparents, and a stray collie or two around the circles painted on the blacktop at Nichols Hills Elementary School. Somehow, Kip and I managed to stay upright until we were in place, the music had changed, and we could blessedly drop hands.

Finally, I heard a familiar voice from weeks of practice: "Put your right foot in..." I fearfully stuck mine forward then scanned the circle...and I had the same foot in as all the smart kids in class. *I did it! I did it right!* The blood fell further back into place as the pounding in my chest receded. "...and shake it all about..." I was shaking and giggling and spinning under the evening sky as the voice instructed, "...Do the Hokey Pokey as you turn yourself around!" Our grand entrance was a grand success! I sang and clapped the finals words, "Do the Hokey Pokey! Do the Hokey Pokey! Do the Hokey Pokey! That's what it's all about!" And it was.

***

A few decades later, I was thumbing through the PBS annual gift catalog. I flipped the page and smiled. I knew the gift that I would buy—and it was for me. The script on the sweatshirt read, "What if the Hokey Pokey really is what it's all about?"

I couldn't help but ponder if the designer was serious or not, whether I should feel discouraged, or called to remember that "all that I ever really needed to know I learned in kindergarten." Or perhaps I only wanted to replay a sentimental moment in my early life when life's biggest challenge was staying upright as I skipped to my first public performance with a large motor skills-challenged genius.

The sweatshirt arrived. I wore it a couple of times, then realized it made me look a bit like a baby elephant. I relegated it to the closet corner of should-be recycled items that had too much sentimental value to make it to Goodwill.

A couple of weeks ago, the pastor at our church embraced the stewardship (ask people for monetary support) season with enthusiasm. He preached on the Old Testament verses from the Book of Esther. Mordecai, Ester's uncle, challenges her not to recoil in fear in a time of great trouble but to see her unlikely marriage, as a Jewish maiden, to the king of the most powerful kingdom in the land, as providence.

"For if you remain silent at this time, relief and deliverance for the Jews will arise from another place, but you and your father's family will perish. And who knows but that you have come to royal position for such a time as this?" (Esther 4:14, New International Version)

Our pastor went on to recount the number of reasons for fear, for discouragement, for frustration, and perhaps desperation as our long economic "recovery" feels more and more like a prolonged illness with a receding hope for cure. He suggested there were plenty of reasons to pull in, hunker down, protect our own and our own turf, and to wrap our arms around ourselves.

Then suddenly, out of the blue, or the gray, he asked us to stand up "if you'd like," not being one to impose musts, shoulds, and have-to's.

"How many of you remember doing the 'Hokey Pokey' as a child?" he asked.

Hands tentatively went up, along with groans and snickers.

"Put your right hand in, put your right hand out," he began, somewhat off-key, and the majority of his congregants obeyed. "Who remembers the words of the final verse?"

Only a few mumbled answers, but I couldn't help myself. I began to sing, "Put your whole self in"...and soon the melody began to unfold with growing strength as a generation of Hokey Pokey-ers joined in. We jumped in, we jumped out, a few spun around, and then we robustly ended with, "That's what it's all about!"

"Okay, sit down. That had absolutely nothing to do with my sermon..." our pastor said with a smile, "I could see a greater than normal number of eyes closing."

We laughed, but also knew there was something more.

"But what if, what if we did put our whole selves in? What if we allowed God to shake up our lives? And what if God used us to turn the world around? What if we are called 'to such a time as this'?"

"What if instead of this," he pulled his arms in around himself, like a self-administered bear hug, "we opened our arms wide?" He spread his arms like condor wings. "What if the Hokey Pokey really is what it's all about?"

I went right home and dug through the back of the closet. *Where is that sweatshirt?* I pulled it out and put it on. I'll never look at it or wear it the same again.

And "that's what it's all about." Thank you, Miss Apostle.

LADY'S MAN

Today while the blossoms still cling to the vine,
I'll taste your 'stwaberries', I'll drink your sweet wine.
A million tomorrows will all pass away,
Ere I forget, all the joy that was mine today.

I'll be a dandy and I'll be a rover,
You'll know who I am by the songs that I sing.
I'll feast at your table, I'll sleep in your clover,
Who cares what tomorrow shall bring.

Randy Sparks

I have only one picture of my maternal grandfather as a young man; Papa is tall and dark with a cigarette hanging from his lips, leaning against a streetcar. My mother used to tell me that I got my long fingers from him, just like she did, and as a child, she liked to place her fingers in the troughs of her father's wavy hair. She also said he had once been quite a lady's man.

The Papa I knew had stooped shoulders that dropped him far below his once six-foot, one-inch frame. He had only a few gray hairs left on top of his balding head, and he wore wire spectacles. No cigarette. No waves. No ladies.

I can't recall any words, either. I can't remember a single conversation between him and Nanny (who talked non-stop to almost everyone else), or between him and *any*one.

The only exception was when he fell in the hallway on the hard, thin carpeting, and mumbled over and over again, "Momma, momma, momma..." I watched with wide eight-year-old eyes and pounding heart until Nanny told me to go call my mother while she cradled his head and assured him, "I'm here, Papa. I'm right here." Later I learned he'd had the first of several "pin strokes."

Papa worked in his shop out back. I went out there a couple of times and stood silently by while he "puttered." I can only recall a couple fruits of his labor.

In my Oklahoma City years, we had a long-handled, metal dust pan that Papa had welded, and Nanny and Papa's house had a child's chair that he had made for my mother when she was a very little girl. I tried to fit into it whenever I visited, but my hips were too wide; I think it was made for size two.

He also puttered in his garden behind the back fence and brought me sun-filled strawberries to dip in a mountain of powdered sugar. In the winter, he frosted my orange halves instead while we waited for strawberries to reappear on the vines.

Papa smoked a pipe. He had a whole row of them on the parlor mantle; some with polished bowls, others with carved heads, all sent by my Uncle Pep from Bavaria. Below them, on the fire screen, hung his cane.

Papa had his own bedroom on the left, down the long hallway leading to Nanny's. (I suppose at one time they'd shared a bed, but in my experience, grandparents had two, and they were no exception.) His "old man" room smelled of dirty socks and week-worn nightshirts—very differently from Nanny's. He had a tall chest of drawers with a honey-colored finish and a short mirror. (Nanny's was a short chest of dark cherry wood with a tall mirror for applying powder and rouge to her high cheekbones.) Papa used Poligrip for his dentures, like other grandfathers, and he watched Mitch Miller while Nanny and I sang along.

He also clipped grass. I suppose he mowed as well, but I only remember him down on his knees edging the driveway with his clippers—a slow and onerous task, I would imagine, in an Oklahoma summer of cicadas and high humidity—but one that kept him busy and out of Nanny's kitchen.

When we got the call from the hospital that Papa had fallen and broken his hip, he had been doing just that—edging the fescue. No one could say how long he had lain there, without a voice, before he was found.

I was quickly warned that a broken hip was often the end for old people, although I couldn't make the connection at all between a broken hip and "the end." But sure enough, in just a few weeks, Papa passed on.

I remember dancing in from a day of play and casually calling out, "How's Papa today?" Daddy quickly covered the phone in his hand, and with his best funeral voice, dark and heavy with compassion, he gave me the news of my first family death. Uncovering the phone, but not changing his tone, he continued making "the arrangements." (My dad was the director of Street & Draper Funeral Home—but not the person who works on bodies, as I was quick to assure those who inquired of his employment.) Papa was gone.

My last memories of Papa were really ones of Nanny and my mother at his funeral. I was soaking my white lace handkerchief with unstoppable tears behind Nanny at All Souls Episcopal Church. She sat under her veiled hat, fingers holding tightly the back of the pew, chin tilted up and cheeks dry.

I whispered to Mother, "Why isn't Nanny crying?"

As if I were old enough to understand, she replied, "Well, marriage to Papa wasn't always easy."

I nodded, feigning comprehension.

Not easy? How could that be true? After all, he was a lady's man.

"MOTHER, YOU SHOULD SEE HOW NICE THAT BATHROOM IS!"

sue nell
ages three to fifteen

Oh give me that good ole mountain dew, yahoo!
And them that refuse it are few, mighty few!
I'll shut up my mug if you'll fill up my jug
With that good ole mountain dew!

Many childhoods have choruses that repeat themselves again and again: the one meant to educate, the one for a good laugh, another to remind us of our manners.

Mine had many. For the unsuspecting dinner guest with no preference when it came to fried chicken parts? "All right, Lula, bring in the feet!" Not quite up to finishing your dinner? "Eat all your potatoes and pea (pee) on your plate!" Innocently ask where John is at? "Just before the 'at'." Accidently refer to children as "kids"? "If I'm a kid, you're a goat and all the slop goes down your throat."

I had my own refrain. I reserved it for the table after the arrival of a PB & J sandwich with the crusts cut off, after the curly fries, after the maraschino cherry from the Shirley Temple, but before the banana split.

When the moment came, I would cross my legs, excuse myself, and head for the back hall of whatever restaurant we were in. Upon my return, I couldn't contain my enthusiasm: "Mother! You should see how nice *that* bathroom is!"

Curiously enough, my greatest dining pleasure for many years was...checking out the restroom.

The restroom at Delores' was dimly lit and a bit sinister with red velvet wallpaper, amber lanterns, and a cigarette machine featuring "Lucky Strikes" hanging just outside the entrance.

But I always met Tweety Bird, my imaginary girlfriend, behind the bathroom door. We would linger long, assuming there was no one else in the next stall, catching up on the latest news.

"Whatcha been up to lately?" I'd ask.

"Oh, not much," she'd say, as she jiggled the handle to make sure the toilet wouldn't run, "just a trip to Disneyland and the Empire State Building."

"Neato."

It was so cool how she always knew when I was coming and would be waiting right next door.

Inevitably, upon my return to the table, all four brothers and my parents would chorus, "What *took* you so long?"

The pink would tinge my ears as I explained, "Oh, I was just talking to Tweety Bird," as if everyone didn't already know. And then I would whisper, "Mother! You should see how nice *that* bathroom is!"

Despite its cafeteria style, Lady Classen had a particularly nice lady's room. There was a lounge area where you could touch up your make-up, powder your nose, or adjust your slip. I could never really imagine someone wanting to hang out in a bathroom lounge, but when there was one, it certainly moved that restroom up on my "Top Ten" list.

Other touches that I looked for: faucets in the shape of a rose, hand-painted sinks, silent flushes, colored commodes, or separate rooms for the throne. My cousin's mother-in-law, Mrs. N, had one in her "boudoir." I discovered it at his wedding reception when everyone was too busy tasting and toasting to notice the extended disappearance of one eight-year-old girl. Mrs. N even had separate compartments for every pair of earrings, and matching shoes to go with her silk pants and matching silk blouses. I longed to spend extra hours in her dressing room doing some in-depth cataloguing.

As I grew, my fascination with bathrooms, or more specifically, toilets, grew also, despite the trauma of having fallen into one in the middle of the night when Daddy left the lid up—again.

My oldest brother, Jack, who by my pre-teen years was making regular intercontinental business trips to Japan and Hong Kong, told me about accidently opening the door on a Japanese woman in an airplane who was seated backwards on an American-style toilet. His blunder totally exploded my toilet-bowl horizons. I had no idea that there were "foreign" WC's, beyond, of course, the outhouses that we frequented with regularity (and irregularity) on summer vacations in Colorado.

We had an outhouse attached to our bunkhouse that Lula, our maid, used, but Daddy preferred the low-tech variety as well. He would go over to Thweatt's cabin each morning for his daily meditation because Ol' Mr. Phelps, Franny Thweatt's daddy, had built a somewhat secluded outhouse with a picture window of Mt. Meeker and Chief's Head—if you left the door open. The Sears' catalogue was rough on the bottom, but the view—wow!

Truth be told, one of the highlights of my youth had been spent with six other stranded fisherpersons during a torrential, deafening downpour near Finch Lake in the Wild Basin sector of Rocky Mt. National Park. We had ridden our mounts up the Allenspark trail for a day of fly fishing, and/or falling in creeks and fishing our flies out of bushes. Daddy was our trip (cheer) leader. He had taught us well to ignore a little "liquid sunshine" or "Rocky Mt. Dew," but when hail began to bounce several feet off the ground and we couldn't count to "one" between lightening strikes and thundering responses (a count of seven equaled a strike a mile away), we started looking for any shelter available. It soon became clear that our only option was the outhouse.

Given my predilections, and a delirious sense of adventure that had struck us all, we piled in. Soon we were singing,

Oh give me that good ole mountain dew, yahoo!
And them that refuse it are few, mighty few!
I'll shut up my mug if you'll fill up my jug
With that good ole mountain dew!

We had one guest, Ellen Records, who wasn't quite familiar with the "lemons to lemonade" theory of Street family outdoor adventures, so we awarded the throne, closed of course, to her.

After all the verses of "This Land is Your Land," "I've Been Workin' on the Railroad," and "Down by the Ole Mill Stream" (which by then was running through the outhouse), we decided it was time to bow to the rain gods, mount our poor, suffering beasts of burden, and get on down the trail. Our steeds needed no encouragement.

We left our shelter behind and sailed towards the horse barn at a swift trot bordering on a dead run. Daddy continued to lead us in song, punctuated by drunken exclamations of "Happy New Year!" without a lick of liquor among us. (Okay, maybe Daddy had had a little "snake bite.") Our rain-filled boots and soggy socks did nothing to detract from one of my best childhood memories.

Beyond outhouses, my toilet familiarity was limited to the "American Standard." I was soon to learn that the good ole U.S. of A. didn't have a corner on toilets anymore than on economic and political systems. Jack had to instruct Mother and Daddy on how to use the Japanese variety when they were going to stay in a traditional Japanese inn on their first and only Asia trip. Soon they were sitting backwards with the best of them.

On my first overseas trip at age fifteen, I was introduced to a peculiar looking, open-with-no-back, pink "toilet" in a Parisian hotel just off the Champs Elysées. It sat in the middle of the room, next to the more recognizable model. I just couldn't figure it out how to use what I later learned was a bidet, and Mother and Dad refused to let me in on "how" or "why." I guess it was just one of those things you didn't talk about, like money or sex.

Later on, during that same trip, Daddy suffered from the traveler's trots. They struck in several exotic (geographical) locations: a tram descending to the glaciers at Chamonix, crammed with camera-toting Japanese tourists; stuck in traffic in a Fiat on our way back to Rome from a beach restaurant with our fist-waving waiter, Amadeus; and under the victorious WWII landmark, the Arc de Triomphe, with all its concentric traffic circles of honking maniacs. (Or so they seemed for someone under gastronomic distress.)

Somehow Daddy faced down death to make it across all seven lanes on foot to a restaurant on the other side, only to discover the *salle de bain* (bathroom) for the *gentilhommes (gentlemen)* was *occupé*. In desperation, and having already survived the onslaught of a thousand Renaults and Citroëns, he ducked inside the one marked with a flowered hat. With sheepish relief, he exited several minutes later to the irritation and arched brows of the *dames* who were waiting none too patiently in line. Mother and I were there with our sympathy, calm and relaxed, having discovered the pedestrian tunnel *under* the roadway.

Despite years of finding "friendly trees" on mountain hikes in Colorado, or succumbing to the nose-pinching, breath-holding experiences of campground outhouses, nothing had prepared me for the bathroom experience I would face in Grenoble, France during my college study-abroad program. The brutality of the bathroom in my brother Bill's fifth-story flat in Grenoble bore no resemblance to those earlier accommodations.

Bill had moved to France post-college, post-inspired year authoring a book on a house boat on the Thames, with his new love, Jane. He harbored some romantic notion of living the desperately poor author's life in the dregs of one of the most spectacularly beautiful places on the planet. (Or maybe he just didn't have much money.)

He and Jane were living on the top floor of a tenement with cobblestones below, multi-colored flowerpots and unrefrigerated milk cartons perched on the open windowsill, and a dozen or so single, male, Moroccan immigrants living down the hall in search of the same rock bottom rent—and next to the only *loo* on the floor.

OUT OF RED DIRT

I had been in France for several months by that point, so I was already adept at balancing on foot grates and squatting over holes that doubled as public restrooms (definitely not on my "Top Ten" list). These, however, did not approach the experience of the bathroom I was to share with Bill's flatmates.

For the first few days, I didn't have to face the full fury of the olfactory storm. Bill would get up early a.m., put on his mailman's wellies, don a full-rubber jacket with hood and elbow-length gloves, arm himself with bucket, brush, and Babo (the 50's equivalent of Comet), and head to the head before Jane and I could crawl from beneath our downy duvets. After the belching, brawling, betting, and beer drinking of the previous night turned to the wee hours of the morn, we could only shudder to think what he might be facing. A half an hour or so later, he would stagger back in and give us the "thumbs up," looking worn and weakened and in need of some seriously stiff coffee.

If I remember correctly, the toilet, shower, and sink were all part of the same space; it was difficult to distinguish where one began and one ended. The "toilet" was as I described previously—a hole in the ground, but it seems like the showerhead hung over it, awkward for showering but great for cleaning.

I was eternally grateful to Bill, especially after one morning when I could wait no longer and I stumbled down the hallway first, only to back away in horror when I opened the door. The white porcelain was barely discernible beneath the brown and yellow stains and drains clogged with thick, black hair. It looked like it hadn't been cleaned in centuries versus the twenty-four hours since Bill had made his last assault. I clutched my stomach. Not wanting to add its contents to the deposits already therein, I turned and ran, my urgent needs forgotten.

As I reached the door of the apartment, Bill was headed out, all dressed in yellow. I would have kissed his feet if I hadn't known where they'd been and where they soon would be.

France and Switzerland went on to introduce me to chain flushes with the reservoir overhead (I had lived a protected life) and, in the Alsatian hills, a shelf with a hole cut through rough boards. It had once hung out over the unsuspecting heads of serfs working the fields, and now over tourists checking out the masonry at the foot of the castle wall, five stories below. *Such luxury for royalty.*

But no other WC approached my Grenoble experience— thank God. Tweety Bird might have boycotted and Mother would have firmly withheld her approved. And, I could not have shared my childhood delight and refrain: "Mother, you should see how nice *that* bathroom is!"

THE CROW'S NEST

O Mister Moon, moon, great big silvery moon,
Won't you please shine down on me?
O Mister Moon, moon, great big silvery moon,
Won't you come from behind that tree, that tree-o?

After the Fourth of July fireworks each year in Oklahoma City, our family headed to Allenspark on the southern flanks of Rocky Mountain National Park. On my first visit, I was three months old. I would return every summer until I turned twelve. Tired of changing tires in the years before radials, tired of sitting on the side of the road in Kansas in August waiting for the tow truck, fed up with liquid air, water moccasins as swimming partners in the Ole Cimarron River, and mountainless views, we relocated for the long term to Allenspark in the summer of '68. No doubt the shaking heads of four sons when offered a future in the funeral business influenced our move as well. Dad sold out and packed up for year-round living on Willow Creek—without hesitation.

But prior to permanent residency, the first thing I would do when we arrived each July was to climb up Cowbell Hill. It was as high as my little legs and lungs could take me on the first day at 8500 feet—about 100 feet elevation gain, I'd say.

The second thing I would do was climb the ladder to the "Crow's Nest"—about eight feet straight up. This was my summer bedroom in Windwhistle, the official name of what we all affectionately referred to as "The Old Cabin."

The Crow's Nest could be reached only by a hand-hewn, pine ladder nailed to fire-burned logs rescued in 1922 by Grandmother and Granddaddy Street. At a total cost of $1398.60, including furnishings, the Old Cabin still stands today on Cowbell Hill, in the shadow of Mt. Meeker—the chief's belly—and Chief's Head...well, er...the chief's head. Estes Cone forms the feet of the ancient granite warrior who lies stretched out on his back in full view, or at least until the ponderosas grew tall enough to block it, of the front porch of Windwhistle.

The Crow's Nest was, and is, the bedroom of each sub-four-foot child whose hands have grown large enough to grasp the fat rungs, but whose legs are still stunted sufficiently to fit into the half-sized, custom-built beds. One chest of drawers rounds out the décor, the kind whose warped sides alternately stick on the left and then the right so that you're forced to yank hard on the metal handles until suddenly, yet not unexpectedly, the entire drawer loses its grip and crashes to the floor.

But the Crow's Nest was primo "propity." Perched in the rafters, behind one-by-eights nailed only as high as a four-year-old's shoulders, you could see and hear all that was transpiring in the two bedrooms, to the left and right, and in the living room, to the front and below. Perhaps that's why Daddy was always grabbing a blanket and suggesting "nature walks" (wink, wink) to Mother.

"Hey Babe, how's 'bout a nature walk?" he'd say, with a little pat to her backside.

I don't remember her verbal response, but proverbial actions speak louder than words. Off they'd go. Took me years before I figured out Mother wasn't really much fond of hiking.

My favorite activity from the Crow's Nest was to climb up the ladder, over the splinter-prone, stunted walls, and onto the top Lincoln Log of the wall surrounding the guest bedroom below. I would stretch my arms out behind me to hold onto the backside of the Nest's boards, measure the dizzying distance, and then leap to the seriously sagging double bed below. Tommy and Bill would usually stand near the bed to keep me from flying off and cracking my head on the cold linoleum floor. I was not the first Street child to practice this feat. Needless to say, the bedsprings were not so good.

Never ones to interfere with clean, honest fun, my parents ignored—or even encouraged—our high-flying stunts. They also ignored chopping down aspen groves, solo hikes across snowfields in a lightning storm, and John Records pushing me off Big Rock, attached by carabiners to a homemade zip line, across a twenty-foot abyss to neighboring Loaf Rock, 100 yards away. I was only eight years old. I laughed so hard I wet my pants. Currently, this style of parenting might be categorized as "gross negligence."

Once, when Mother and Daddy were away fishing on Coney Creek, Jack, my oldest brother, put me in a trunk and spun me around on the marbled-green linoleum floor that had been a late addition to the Old Cabin to protect crawling knees and bare feet from infectious splinters. The floor was the perfect surface for spinning. Great fun.

Next, he and a friend hoisted me up the ladder to the Crow's Nest—not quite so much fun. My heart rate increased and moisture began to frizz my pin curls. Adults would recognize this as panic or claustrophobia. But I could hear the boys' hysterical laughter and assumed this was supposed to be delirious amusement for me as well.

Lastly, they positioned Tommy and Bill below at their usual posts. When it finally registered what was about to happen, it was too late to scream. They threw me over the top of the stunted walls and I bounced higher than ever before. Well, at least the trunk did. My face resembled mashed potatoes as it smashed into the lid's wooden slats. When all my body parts settled back into their original positions, and I realized that I had survived, I joined in their gut-splitting glee.

Just to prove he wasn't such a bad guy after all, Jack lugged me outside, hefted me, trunk and all, to the roof of the station wagon, and showed off his recently acquired driving skills as he careened round and round the road circling the Old Cabin.

When the gravel stopped flying, I crawled out of the luggage, took a few dizzied steps, and found myself none the worse for wear with a good story intact.

We Streets are always ones for a good story.

***

But what I liked most about the Crow's Nest were rainy days knocking on the roof and losing myself in a Hardy Boys or Nancy Drew mystery in my four-foot bed. Or warm summer nights when the heat from the day and the fireplace stones rose to my hideaway. I would open the screenless window and shrink beneath the diamond-studded velvet of a million lights, wondering just where God was up there and feeling very, very,

very small. I would call to Mister Moon and then whisper to him quietly, all the while comforted by the crackle and sighs of evening below.

-13-

A DARK AND STORMY NIGHT

Dark one night, when we were all in bed,
Old Mother Leary left the lantern in the shed
And when the cow kicked it over,
She winked her eye and said,
"There'll be a hot time in the old town, tonight!"

"It was a dark and stormy night...and three men were sitting around the campfire..."

The cadence of Gramps' voice began slowly—then quickened. It rose, drawing nearer the faces of his five children, along with a hodgepodge of first-time visitors and a scattering of seasoned adults.

"...The first man's name was Mo, the second Jo, and the last, Gus Gunderson. And the first man turned to the second and said..."

Gramps stopped abruptly. He held us rapt with his bushy raised brows and slighted parted lips that withheld the next line. The rain drummed on the rooftop, crescendoing as we crouched and huddled near the open hearth of the floor-level fire in the Old Cabin. We leaned in further, eyes as big as the black-iron frying pan hanging on the kitchen wall. As stray cinders popped and whistled towards the worn and frayed hooked rug, the youngest rushed to stamp them out while the rest waited in the taut interlude...

Finally, Little Nell could wait no longer, "What did he say, what did he say?" she asked.

We all moved to the fringe of the rug or the edge of our pine board benches. Gramps tensed and teased a few seconds more. And then, "It was a dark and stormy night... and three men sat around the campfire," he concluded.

"But what happened next?" we all cried together, even those of us who knew this telling by heart.

***

Was there an answer? Was there a fantasmic unfolding befitting the night? How long did we wait for the resolution? Was this the climax? Was there no punchline?

My memory stops with Gus. I've probed my brothers' as well, but none can deliver a more satisfying conclusion. Why do we all remember the race of our heartbeats and the silence of our suspended breaths? Why do we all gather our own children on starless nights, light a match, set the logs on fire, break out the marshmallows, graham crackers, Hershey's, and long blackened forks? And why do we all repeat, "And one man turned to the other and said..."?

Because...because we were all swept up in, or better yet, joint tenants of Gramps' mythical tales. We begged for them again and again as the wind whistled through the pines and under the door of the Old Cabin on Cowbell Hill. And though we were not satisfied, we forgave his torture and forgot his betrayal when soon our imaginations were distracted by flaming treats.

Not long, and we'd ask for a different kind of story: "Gramps, let's sing 'Down by the Ole Mill Stream.'"

We started slow then doubled the tempo, oldsters carrying the first line, youngsters following with clarifications: "Down by the ole (not the new but the ole), mill stream (not the river but the stream)." Next we warmed up further with a rambunctious rendition of "Do Lord, O Do Lord, O do ya 'member me?", little ones grinning with hands raised high on the hallelujahs. When it came time for "Swing Low, Sweet Chariot," we all knew our parts; we knew our roles: which voices would rise on the high notes, which would pick up the base, who would clap and who would provide the tempo with a steady foot-stomping on the splintered floorboards.

OUT OF RED DIRT

My favorite song was Gramps' as well. "Daddy, do 'Dark One Night When We Were All in Bed'...please!" He'd sing the first verse and I'd join him on the second—the backwards version: "Night one dark, when bed we all in were, Old Leary Mother left the shed in lantern door...," all the way to the end, "...there'll be a time hot in the town old, night to!"

***

The Old Cabin was my second childhood home—now it's my only one. Every summer until I was twelve, we abandoned the red dirt and sweltering, tar-melting heat of Oklahoma City for the cool, crisp fragrance of Rocky Mountain afternoons. When I turned twelve, we stayed. Gramps and Nan built a year-round home not far from the Old Cabin on Willow Creek. I lived there until I left for college, and returned for Christmas' through 1979. On January 31, 1980, with four feet of snow on the ground and roof, and the closest fire hydrant twenty miles away, the furnace exploded. The propane bills had been particularly high that winter, due to a leak rather than the high winds and low temperatures as once imagined, so one spark— and up she went. The flames refused to relent until only a twenty-five foot chimney and half a garage still stood. Nan escaped with literally the shirt on her back, and Gramps and

Delilah, his beloved keeshond, arrived from the dump only in time to see Nan exiting the blackened front door.

After the fire, only the Old Cabin remained. But it was enough. It *is* enough.

***

The Street cabin was the first to arrive on Cowbell Hill. It hosts a west view of snowy peaks, a kitchen whose drawers and cabinets regularly reveal mouse droppings and garbage scattered by the daily visits of nocturnal ninjas, and a primitive bathroom that, until recently, could only provide for one-and-a-half baths in its clawfoot tub before dousing you with ice-water. After a bone-drenching day fishing at Pear Lake, followed by a bone-bouncing return on horseback and a narrow escape from lightning bolts and golf ball-sized hail, it was always a race to see who would get the first, and only, soak.

At night in the Old Cabin you can appreciate the evening stars through gaps in the chinking around the stone chimney. They also lend themselves to migrant mammals seeking a softer way of life. I remember well the time Gramps was racing from bedroom to living room and back again, broom in hand, chasing a winged vampire that had almost touched down on Nan's bristled rollers. She covered her head with both arms as I screamed, "Where is it? Where is it?" Before anyone could say, the bat was no more.

Nails of different shapes and sizes pierce the Old Cabin's knotty walls. A soft, misshapen, gray felt cowboy hat with a leather band rests on one—on another hangs the cracked straw Stetson that Gramps wore with his Wrangler jacket and jeans. For years I rode behind him on an appaloosa named Ranger as I followed his worn elbows and cigarette smoke up the Allenspark Trail or along Ski Road. He'd raise his arm, threads flapping in the wind, to signal us when it was time for a full gallop or when to slow for approaching riders.

The jacket now hangs to the left of the entry to the bedrooms, a note tucked in its breast pocket. It's a note to my brother Bill, a bequest of Gramp's favorite cabin wear to the one he knew would sew up the seams, patch the tears, and join his memory with each cast of a fly on the North Saint Vrain River or near the inlet at Pear Lake.

***

Over the desk stands a handsome young couple—both with balloon riding pants tucked into knee-high leather boots and Roy Rogers/Dale Evans hats shading their wide grins and eyes. The 1934 photo was snapped just outside the Old Cabin door, a sun-faded Mt. Meeker as its backdrop. Gramps was nineteen-years-old and Nan seventeen, just six years from the day in 1928 when he offered a friend twenty-five cents to introduce him to little Nell Phillips. He was smitten from that day forward and you can still see it in his eyes.

Next to the couple, a big-bosomed grandmother kneels behind five grandsons in matching plaid shirts, all stitched by her skilled hands. Tommy is the youngest with chubby cheeks that match his grandmother's. A few feet away and next to the front door, the seven Streets of my immediate family, Gramps and Nan, four older brothers, and my three-year-old self, squint in the noon-day sun, perched or leaning on a white stockade fence at nearby Cheley Colorado Camps. I was scared, that day, of the photographer with the Albert Einstein hair that tried forever to get me to smile.

But there are more stories on the walls. Year after year, the one behind the moth-eaten shirt in the corner with the porcupine quills passes on to the youngest heir or newest visitor.

"Gramps chased the varmint across the road, took off his shirt, and tried to capture the thing to take home to his mother—just knew she'd love it, but the porkie would have nothing of it. He escaped, leaving behind the better part of his quills."

Gramps' namesake, John Gordon Street, Jr., tried the same trick years later with his fishing vest. It hangs nearby.

***

The first family member to arrive each year, almost never before June because any earlier and the ground is frozen and the pipes still in danger, must face winter's ravages. Pine needles litter the living room floor, swept in by seventy-five mile per hour west winds, and no doubt, a pack rat or two who has built a nest in the wood box or under the kitchen sink. (Just ask Ella Street who had to stare one down in the spring of 2011.) Out comes the Windex to unmask the evening sunsets over Mt. Tanima, and the horseshoes get hung on a nail in the ponderosa, just feet from the front porch so a crowd can cheer competitors from their rocking chairs.

In the corner, above the faded green and red plaid window seat covers, a series of simple shelves climb the wall. They must be dusted. But this involves moving a pair of miniature cowboy boots worn by each toddler who visits. I believe my nephew, Bryan Street, a few years shy of fifty, was the first to wear these. My little white ones have disappeared, but they were quite famous in their day.

I remember when I wore them home for the first time. We arrived in Colorado on the second day past the Fourth of July each year. After an overnight in Lamar—just over the Oklahoma-Colorado border and another six hours, forty degrees fall in temperature, and a five thousand foot climb to "God's Country"—we'd make our way to the Old Cabin via Limon, Longmont, and Lyons. Allenspark, however, was grocery-less in those days, so we endured a final stop at the supermarket in Longmont, resenting the delay despite our stomachs' demands. We loaded a month's worth of groceries into the back of the already overloaded Mercury station wagon—the back bumper grazing the ground. Nan and Gramps, a handful of kids, Lula, our maid, and Delilah and Sampson, our keeshonds in heavy fur coats, tested the shocks way beyond their endurance point.

After an eternal fifty minute drive, leaning left and right into our human and canine neighbors, our noses recognized the vanilla scent of massive ponderosas mixed with a cocktail of early summer blossoms: lupine, Rocky Mountain columbine, mariposa lilies, and fragile harebells. "We're here!" we all shouted as we passed the sign advertising the Street, Ludlow, Parker, Henry, and Thweatt cabins.

Before the afternoon rains fell at the strike of four, we had already taken our first hike up Cowbell Hill and begun the annual clean-up of the Old Outcamp, first built with fallen aspens by Great Uncle Bob Allen, Aunt Mary Louise, and Gramps when they were youngsters.

When I was three, the morning after our arrival began like all the others. My parents and older siblings busied themselves with stocking the pantry shelves, sanitizing the silverware drawer and its contents after discovering rodent residue, and freeing stale linens from their winter hibernation under the window seats and in cedar chests. Despite their mothball-laced encasements, a few more holes had appeared in the scratchy woolen blankets and thinning quilts.

While Bill and Tommy, my two youngest brothers, swept up mountains of moth wings and dead flies, I wandered off Cowbell Hill along the trail which led into "downtown" Allenspark, maybe twenty buildings—tops. This was in the days before construction of the new Highway 7 had scoured and scorched the hillside separating the Old Cabin from the town center. It involved quite a trek for a three-year-old.

I never made it past my first stop: a semi-social visit with Cecil and Pearl (*Missus* and *Mister*) Sinn at SINN'S Western Trail. The west side of the store housed Cecil's collection of musty antiques, of little interest to a three-year-old. The east side showcased both fishing gear and western wear. Gramps seldom purchased his flies and tackle from Pearl—he suspected

Pearl regularly tipped off the forest ranger as to the time, date, and route of his return from alpine lakes from whence his creel would predictably carry a few more than his limit.

But the western wear attracted me. On that July morn, a pair of little white cowboy boots with red stitching caught my eye.

"Hi, Mrs. Sinn, how are you today?" I began.

"Well, well, who do we have here? It if isn't Little Miss Sue Nell," Cecil said, "another year older and almost all grown up! Welcome back to Allenspark."

"Why thank you, Mrs. Sinn," I said, eyes focused on the boots.

"What brings you in today?" she asked.

"I wanted to say 'hi' to you and Mr. Sinn...and my parents want me to have those little white cowboy boots."

Mrs. Sinn's eyebrows rose before her question. "Oh they do, do they?"

"Yes, they do. You can just put them on our account," I assured her.

I could tell when she glanced quickly at Mr. Sinn, who momentarily replaced his near-permanent scowl with a chuckle, that she wasn't quite convinced. My confidence persuaded her nonetheless. She rang up the boots, made a note in her tin recipe box, put my Keds in a sack, and sent me off up the hill.

It's not easy walking in cowboy boots on a dusty trail that has been plowed by horses' hooves and mined with chipmunk holes and cow pies, but somehow I managed. When I got within sight of the humming bird feeders hanging from the eaves of the Ludlow cabin, I dusted off my prize purchases, adjusted my cowboy hat, and wiped my hands on my jeans. The screen on the backdoor slammed as I made my entry. Everyone looked up from their chores, snatched from their daydreams.

"Hey everybody, whatcha think of my new little white cowboy boots? Aren't they pretty?"

My dad spoke first. "They sure are, L'il Babe. Where d'ya get those?"

Mother squinted her eyes and tightened her jaw. I maintained a cheerful smile and said, without a hint of self-doubt, "I got'em from Mrs. Sinn. She sure is a nice lady."

"You did, did ya. Well, how did you pay for them?" Daddy asked, undistracted by my "nice lady" comment.

"I put them on our account."

With that, I spun around on my still slick soles and headed for my horse on the front porch. I was listening, but no one said a word.

***

From the top-corner shelf in the Old Cabin, above the little boots and a pair of silver spurs, peer the vigilant six eyes of a flop-eared ouzel goozle and those of his two friends, the wampus pussy and ankus-rankus. To less knowledgeable observers, these animals might resemble the skeletal remains of more familiar fauna: a coyote, a cottontail, or an old cow (for, indeed, there must have been one of the latter at some point—this being *Cow*bell Hill and all). But the blue, red, and green coloring are a dead giveaway that these bones do not belong to just any ordinary species.

While my memory fades regarding the peculiarities of the six-eyed flop-eared ouzel goozle and the ankus-rankus—and though I must admit I'm tempted to make something up—the behaviors of the wampus pussy still remain firmly fixed in my brain.

On dark and stormy nights, Gramps would often recall stories of this once furry friend, along with those of Mo, Jo, and Gus. The wampus pussy has an unusual corporal structure that has developed after years, perhaps centuries, even millennium, of wandering on Cowbell Hill. I say "has" because, of course, the wampus pussy still lives on, though rarely seen. It is a particularly shy creature, and limits most of its above-ground activity to post-midnight excursions. Nan and Gramps reported catching a glimpse of one once during one of their "nature walks." Thus, Gramps was able to give a firsthand account of the wampus pussy's behavior and corresponding physical adaptations.

The wampus pussy is the only animal known to have shorter legs on the uphill side of its body than on the downhill. This is an especially useful combination for a critter that lives out its entire existence on an incline, but it does require it to travel in only one direction while facing forward, clockwise on the south-facing slope, counterclockwise on the north. It can, however, go in the other direction if willing to walk backwards. The downside is that wampus pussies are a bit more vulnerable to attack because they can't see where they are going while in reverse, and can't turn on their heels and run.

Wampus pussies also have a serious problem when they arrive at a ridge. But once again, Nature has come to the rescue: the wampus pussy merely waits patiently until a potential mate arrives from the other side of the hill (a cousin, no doubt, but a cousin will have to do), woos him or her, forms a temporary union, so to speak, and waits nine weeks for their offspring to be born with legs of equal length. This new creature is known as a "ridgerunner." It can continue along the ridge in either direction, but can never leave it. Sadly, much like a mule, it cannot reproduce either, and is left to fend for itself when its parents return to their original homes, stumbling backwards over the cow pies.[1]

Needless to say, at a certain age, I challenged Gramps on the verity and accuracy of his wampus pussy story, but as an adult, I have embraced, and now documented, his eyewitness account.

---

[1] There is some speculation that a ridgerunner, in the distant past, followed a ridge all the way to the ocean's edge. There it discovered and fell in love with a steelhead trout. Interestingly, the steelhead's Latin name is "oncor hynchus," only a slight variation from the modern-day "ankus-rankus." Could the wampus pussy and ankus-rankus be related? Further DNA testing will have to be performed as soon as a live, or recently deceased, specimen is captured. Keep your eyes out and report any sightings to your local Department of Fish and Wildlife. This updated information was provided by William Allen Street, media specialist and fly-fisherperson.

-14-

THE TALK

Billy and Susie sitting in a tree,
K-I-S-S-I-N-G.
First come love, then comes marriage,
Then comes Billy in the baby carriage.

Traditional jump rope rhyme

One evening, during the winter of my fifth grade year, Mother, Daddy, and I sat in front of the black and white Motorola watching Doris Day. I was perched on the arm of our sofa with perfect balance while Mother and Daddy sat holding hands on the plaid cushions.

And then—I fell off...into still, deep waters.

"What does 'Modess' (only I pronounced it 'modest') mean?"

"Oh," my mother offered, without taking her eyes off Doris, "that's when someone doesn't want you to know of his achievements." (Notice that she carefully avoided other meanings, like when you don't want anyone to see you *naked*.)

"No, I don't mean *that* kind of modest. I mean the kind you see on the dispenser in the restroom at Dolores," (our Sunday night, "I don't want to cook" restaurant).

Both sets of eyes, wide with surprise and panic, abruptly left Doris' and locked on mine.

Long seconds tiptoed past.

Mother was first to recover, "Oh, *that* kind of modest. Only it's pronounced 'mo-*dess*', with the stress on the second syllable."

"Yeah, well, what is it?"

If Daddy hadn't been caught totally off-guard, he wouldn't have volunteered for this conversation. He would have excused himself to change a light bulb or mow the lawn or one of a million other tasks usually left to Booker, the yardman, or Oliver, the handyman, whom he dragged home from work from time to time when a chore required technical skills—or any skill.

But he was caught. I heard him suck air all the way to the bottom of his lungs and hold it there, pathetic eyes pleading with my mother to go first. After all, this was *her* part of the deal. He was in charge of "The Talk" with the boys (most of whom claim it never happened), and Mother was supposed to handle me.

Knowing what I do now as a mother of four, I realize that my parents could have stopped at milepost one with their explanation. For some reason, they decided to press on all the way to the cairn atop Mt. Whitney. Maybe there was no decision involved. Maybe they just put one foot in front of the other and, with "never say die" Street family perseverance, they marched ahead, determined to plant their conquering flag at the top of the highest peak, not one step short. Or, maybe, having already answered the "Modess" questions of my older brothers, they just threw all caution to the wind. Why the heck not? Or, maybe, they understood that this was the moment to clear the trail so they could address the *real* issues on the horizon: "first comes love, then comes marriage, then comes Johnny in the baby carriage."

In any case, forward we went; I with an empty backpack, they with a loaded one that they unloaded mile by mile into my own.

First, I heard the simple biology of menstruation, and thus the need for "Modess" or "Kotex" or when you had more experience, "Tampax," (but that was only for advanced, usually married, women. I suspect that my mother was concerned that Tampax might make it impossible to determine virginity on the wedding night.)

At this point, Daddy jumped in and told me why all of us Street grandchildren had inherited Tampax stock. (I knew it sounded vaguely familiar, beyond the blue box tucked in my mother's dressing table drawer.)

"Granddaddy Street thought he was 'buying the future' with *Kodex* stock, a washing machine manufacturer when washing machines were a rather new commodity in American homes. He got the names confused, but it turned out to be a bonanza!"

(After all, in 1967, Tampax was the only company making tampons. The stock split several times, yet kept on rising. Several of my brothers cashed in at the height of Tampax's rocket rise. But in typical Street, hands-off, "surely this will go on forever" fashion, I waited to sell my portion until 1981 when the one-product company's stock had plummeted to a tenth of its peak value. The proceeds were only enough for my husband and me to go to England and buy dress shirts at Marks & Spencer for his first real job.)

Interesting perhaps, but I was not easily distracted by Daddy's stock report...and my backpack still rested featherlike on my shoulders.

"So why do women have to menstruate?" I asked.

Mother picked up the storyline, which inevitably involved babies, nourishing babies, growing babies, and making babies. Looking up, we were already three quarters the way up the mountain! But now for the steep part; there was no turning back.

Mother continued, "So the sperm from the father joins the mother's egg and that's called conception, the beginning of a new life!"

You could see the excitement in her eyes and perhaps a touch of pride for having climbed all the way to this viewpoint calmly, maturely, and using the "real" terms—pretty impressive for a mother and dad in the late sixties. (The following year, my dad was the *only* father out of all three sixth-grade classes to come to the sex-talk night sponsored by the PTA.) By the smug looks on their faces, I'm pretty sure they thought it was time to plant the flag.

But then came the moment none of us had been waiting for and for which I, least of all, was prepared.

"So how does the father's sperm get to the mother's egg?" I asked.

(I can imagine my father saying "D*mn!" under his breath at this point, except he never said "D*mn!"... Okay, maybe once.)

My mother forged ahead with steely determination.

"Well, the father places his penis inside the mother's vagina and the sperm comes out and fertilizes the..."

"What?" I interrupted. "What the heck! You've got to be kidding me. Really? That's just soooooo gross!"

Silence. They both looked a little taken back, a little sheepish, a little guilty; that perhaps they had let the cat out of the bag a bit too soon. After all, I was only eleven.

Doris Day might as well have died. Nobody knew she was still flirting in the background. They waited, fidgeting—Dad with his Naval Academy ring, Mother with the lipstick she kept in her pocket for frequent touch-ups.

"So," I began, avoiding their eyes, "How does it..." (very long pause) "...feel?"

This was too much for my mother. She floundered. But Daddy stepped up in "mountain man" fashion, albeit a tad timidly. He wrinkled his nose, tilted his head to the side and down so that he had to strain to look at me from under his bushy eyebrows, and then, with an abbreviated chuckle, he sucked in his breath, "Well," (long pause) "kinda nice."

Two sets of eyes fell to the shag-rug tundra. Mother studied the ground carefully while I squirmed under the load of my pack.

Was this really the top?

I leaned over to pick up the forgotten flag. I examined it dubiously.

And then with a shrug and a "Why the heck not?" tossed to the wind, I planted it firmly beneath the firmament.

Kinda nice.

JUST AROUND THE NEXT BEND

Down by the Ole (not the new, but the ole)
Mill stream (not the river, but the stream)
That's where I first (not last, but first)
Met you (not me, but you).

It was there (not here, but there)
I knew (not thought, but knew)
That you loved (not hated, but loved)
Me, too (not one, but too).

Tell Taylor

The fire had been lying low all summer. Lightning strikes in June near Ouzel Lake in Rocky Mountain National Park had set off some sleepers. The "let-burn" policy of the national park system forbid any attempt to put them out, and anyway, a bit of housecleaning would be a good thing.

Late in August, wind-whisked sparks ignited the waiting tender and suddenly the sleepers were a raging fire. The sun hung intermittently orange and brown behind billowing columns of smoke in Wild Basin, soon closed except to hundreds of firefighters. One finger of fire snaked its way towards the southern boundary. Nearby stood summer cabins and year-round houses, equally vulnerable to indiscriminate flames—nearby stood our home.

The Park Service, in a last minute attempt to assuage the anxieties of local residents, brought in bulldozers and cut a twenty-foot swath where the Park butted up against private lands. Along with the Allenspark fire department, my dad and I perched nearby on Boundary Line Rock, on lookout for spot fires in front of the advancing edge.

Daddy had never been too good at watching and waiting. It was a family tradition to "be where the action was." Radio chatter put the fire at two miles away. We decided to walk up the Allenspark trail, just a bit, for a better view.

We headed out at a slow pace due to Daddy's "old leg." As we neared the ridge-top, smoke obscured the basin below. I asked, "Should we go any further?"

"Just a little bit further...just around the next bend."

We headed downhill, just a little bit, mind you, quickly reaching the first viewpoint. No fire, no flames, no firefighters. I checked with Daddy again.

"Well," he hesitated, "just a little further...just around the next bend."

This refrain was not new to me. It had been invoked many times in response to an impatient child's query on a long road trip: "Are we there yet?"

Without fail I would hear: "Just a little further, just around the next bend."

Of course, it was never "just around the next bend"—maybe five or six or ten or twelve—but never the next. Regardless, on that otherwise peaceful afternoon, I trusted my daddy once again, and followed him faithfully down the mountain.

We had now rounded several bends in the direction of Calypso Cascades where the Allenspark trail intersects the main one rising from Wild Basin campground. Suddenly, we heard crackling. I looked downhill—no fire. My eyes met Daddy's. He was doing a very good job of disguising the panic we both felt. We looked uphill. Not ten yards away, the Ouzel Lake fire was consuming the spot we had just crossed. What should we do?

Up? "We'll never outrace it on my old leg," Daddy answered before I asked. *Down?* We had no idea what we might find. *Another branch of the fire? Were we trapped?*

"Let's go down," he directed, with the feigned confidence of a professional outdoorsman.

We took off as fast as our three good legs could carry us. More smoke, but no fire. *Could we get to water? Could we reach the other entrance?* No time for debate. The "up" choice had been gobbled as we pondered.

We arrived at the falls without another face-to-face with flames—and without a trace of another face. We had no idea where the fire was except that it had now sealed the trail that had led us from Allenspark to "a better view." We aimed for the Wild Basin campground and hoped for the best.

Soon Daddy had turned a life-threatening event into a laughter-filled adventure. Except for a deserted national park, it appeared we were taking a stroll along the North St. Vrain River on a late summer day whose crispness hinted of autumn.

Not far into our laughter, we looked up at the shocked face of a yellow-jacketed forest ranger with helmet, high boots, hatchet, and hand-held radio. He was charging up the empty trail, nearly falling over himself. He braked suddenly when he saw and old man and young girl casually strolling down the otherwise deserted path.

"What on earth are you doing here?" he yelled. "The entire Park has been sealed off. How did you get here?"

I rushed to explain, but Daddy cut me off, "Well—why, sir? Is there a problem?"

"Yes, there's a problem! There's a forest fire! Where did you come from?"

A twinkle in Daddy's eyes.

Oh no, here comes one of his tall-tale lies—side-splitting in most situations—not in this one.

"Oh, we just hiked over Boulder-Grand Pass (13,000 plus feet) from Grand Lake (fifteen plus miles). We had no idea."

I couldn't believe it. How *could* he?

The ranger's eyes grew wide with alarm. "You need to get out of the Park right now!"

"Yes, sir, we'll do that."

He took off up the trail. We took off down.

Just around the next bend, I exclaimed, "How could you say that, Daddy? Don't do that again! You're gonna get us in *big* trouble."

A sheepish grin.

Not another mile had passed when the same scene replayed itself. I tried a bit harder to apologize for my dad and to excuse his inappropriate attempt to be humorous in a "very serious situation," but I'm not sure whom the ranger believed in the end. He sent us on down the trail as he raced up.

We arrived at the campground twenty years before a cell phone. We consoled ourselves on the extra five-mile walk out the road to civilization with more laughter, a few rounds of

"Down by the Ole Mill Stream," and mutual assurance that this would at least make a great story for years to come.

When a neighbor arrived in his truck to retrieve us, we didn't get a chance to tell it.

"So I hear you went on a little walk through the Park from Grand Lake today," he said.

Daddy and I looked at each other with surprise and more than a little disappointment.

"Yep, came over the fire radio," he added. "'Old man with a flat top and a young girl coming down the trail from Calypso Cascades.' We knew it had to be you."

As I drifted off to sleep against Daddy's shoulder on the way home, I mumbled, "Are we there yet?"

"Just a little bit further, just around the next bend."

ADVENT, 1979

How silently, how silently,
The wondrous gift is given,
How love imparts through human hearts the wonders of His
heaven.

O Little Town of Bethlehem

Advent of 1979 began eight months and twenty days into my second pregnancy with "Rufus," Gramps' name for my unborn child. Gramps, my dad, was twenty days into a diagnosis of lymphoma, and ten days post-surgery for a grapefruit-sized tumor in his colon. My mind, body, and emotions were otherwise focused on a new birth and new beginnings, but they were also darkened with anxiety, fear, and the probable death that was part of a prognosis for lymphatic cancer in 1979.

The day before his due date, Rufus' impatience matched my own. Labor pains burst through the door without a knock...yet retreated when I arrived at the hospital. For twenty-four hours I waited, walked, chatted, and fasted. But when nothing had happened by the next evening, the doctor checked his date book and suggested, "I could move things along a little by…breeching the dam."

"Huh? I said.

"You know, I could break your waters."

Despite my commitment to no outside interference in the birthing process, it was, in fact, Rufus' due date. I decided this one little exception could be overlooked. "Be my guest," I said.

One hour twenty minutes later I was pushing. On the second "effort" (kind of like the "little sting" that doctors often refer to—multiplied by fifty), Ryan Lee Phillips was born, December 10, 1979, at 10:20 p.m.

The lights were dim in the birthing room and all strangers had exited. Jose held Ryan in his arms. Ryan held his daddy in the deep well of his newborn eyes. "Hello, little fella," Jose whispered, and all three of us were enveloped with the peace of love's embrace.

***

Within twenty-four hours, we were on our way home. Our older son, Bryce, age two and a half, reminded us that we hadn't yet decorated a Christmas tree. So with the thermometer measuring negative ten degrees, and the wind chill bringing it to negative thirty, we braked at a local tree farm, Jose leapt from the car, and I pointed. He grabbed a nice bushy spruce, tied it to the top of our Toyota Corolla, and off we went to our three-month-old home in Steven's Point, Wisconsin.

Within days, I learned an important lesson about having two children instead of one: don't leave them alone together in the house, even for a minute.

On Jose's first day back at work, I put on my snow boots under my gown and robe, and traipsed through two feet of snow to the mailbox. When I returned, I found the kitchen door locked...so were the front door and the sliding door and all the windows. Shivering in my boots on the back steps, I tried to teach a two-year-old how to turn and twist the little button thingy in the middle of the doorknob...to no avail. *What to do?*

I saw only one car at home in the neighborhood. My next-door-neighbor was a pastor whom I had not yet met, and he was probably home writing one of his Advent sermons in anticipation of Christmas, only two weeks away. I started to imagine being turned in for child abuse, or at least jailed for stupidity, but it was my swiftly numbing nose and fingers that convinced me to go knock on his door.

A giant of a man with soft, slightly creased eyes, answered. His face did not betray what I was sure were his thoughts: *What in the world is this teenager with two children doing out running around in her nightie on a frozen December morning?* (I was, in fact, twenty-four, but my freckles and diminutive size had led more than one person to label me a "teen mom.") Instead, his response was one of unseasonable Easter grace.

"Of course," he answered, when I asked if I could use his phone to call my husband. And then he offered to go keep Bryce occupied while I explained my dilemma to Jose, at work, ten miles away.

When I got back to the house, the door was open. (I hate to fulfill gender stereotypes, but I received a mere sixteen percent on tool identification and an eleven percent on spatial cognition on the *Armed Forces' Skills Assessment* in high school. Evidently, Mr. Pastor's door-opening explanation was easier for a toddler to decipher than my own.) I ran inside to head off Jose, but he'd already left when I called. Ugh!

Two days later, my "never-leave-them-alone" lesson was reinforced. I had ventured out with both children to the grocery store—a daring adventure with one child, brainless with two. When I returned, I brought in the car seat first, with Ryan aboard, and set it on the living room floor. Bryce trotted in behind. I returned to the car for the groceries, but as I neared the kitchen door, I heard a full-throttle blubbering coming from the living room that clearly did not signal, "I'm hungry." I dropped the potatoes and peas, rushed in, and found Bryce with a delighted grin on his face, singing on top of the upside-down car seat. Ryan hung suspended by the straps, face down.

***

Christmas was only a week away when Gramps called with a cancer-weakened voice and asked for Jose. I knew something was up.

"Could Sue Nell and the boys possibly come to Colorado for the holidays? We'll pay, of course. I'm so sorry, but I'm not quite back up on my feet after the surgery, and both chemo and radiation are on the menu for the New Year. We'll come out there next year."

"Of course," Jose said, despite facing Christmas "home alone." He hadn't been at his new job long enough to ask for days off.

I have to admit I was a bit nervous about flying with a two-week-old baby and a toddler, but both passengers and flight crew helped me on and off the plane, assisted my transfer in Minneapolis, and kept Bryce entertained while I nursed Ryan. I also brought along a full-metal jacket of grapes, cheerios, wooden puzzles, and a worn copy of *Where the Wild Things Are* for my little "wild thing" should he "roar his terrible roar" or "gnash his terrible teeth."

***

We landed safely in Denver. Bill, my youngest brother, and his wife Jane had already arrived, all the way from Bristol, England—easy as pie. Tom flew in from Germany, Jim and family arrived via Volvo from Seattle within minutes of their projected time, stopping only for pre-determined bladder breaks. And of course, the oldest, Jack, who lived forty-five minutes away, had already begun his year-long journey of care and compassion for Dad.

A neighbor picked us up at Stapleton Field. As we headed northwest to the mountains, we had no trouble on I-25, or even on the section from Longmont to Lyons. But as we began to climb on Hwy 7, along the South St. Vrain River, past the coral cliffs, nearly to the Riverside turn-off (where Dad never wanted to live because it was "down in the gulley"), more and more snow filled the boughs and dressed the hillsides with an oversized white coat. It spilled onto the roadway, sending us this way and that.

As we topped the hill above Ferncliff, the storybook land of Allenspark in winter embraced us. Smoke rose from the chimneys of year-round residents and mixed with the pungent smell of frozen ponderosa beneath Mt. Meeker, second highest peak in Rocky Mountain National Park.

At the crest, the sky's arms opened wide. Across the valley was Home. I could see Big Rock where soon we would fly off our tubes and brush the ice from our brows below the old ski jump, tumble out of our toboggan on Suicide Hill (missing *most* of its trees) then dig out the Ski Doo on the Big Curve as we tried to race back up to the top for another run.

Minutes later, as I propped open the front door of my late childhood home with a hip, one babe in arms and the other in a backpack, I was greeted by bows and red berries on the mantle. Beside a cornucopia wreath rose a seventeen-foot-high Christmas tree that Gramps had probably scoped out months ago to meet Nan's, my mother's, exacting standards. (But it had been most likely felled more recently by Jack as he quietly picked up Dad's axe to provide this year's centerpiece.)

Cousin Wilda's dolls hid deep in the branches, Tommy's angel, perched on top, sang above golden tinsel strung alongside popcorn and cranberries. To my left was the manger of all my Christmases past. Baby Jesus was not yet there among the usual cast of characters in the hand-made shed of sticks and straw. He would arrive mysteriously sometime

Christmas Eve. I stumbled in with another infant child cradled in the crook of my elbow.

But not for long. Gramps appeared suddenly amidst all the other aunts, uncles, cousins, and an unfamiliar, yet welcoming puppy. Despite the pallor on his cheeks and unusual slowness in his step, there was a bright light in his eyes. "Hello, little f-f-fella." His voice cracked as he held his twelve-day-old grandson for the first time, tears following close behind.

At six o'clock on Christmas Eve, the whole family gathered for the service at St. James on the Mount. There was little doubt we would take up half the pews of the community church built with fire-burned logs from the thirties.

On cue, snow began to fall as we bundled up in newly knitted hats and mittens, down parkas, and knee-high boots for the trek down the road into the center of Allenspark. Ryan was swallowed up inside the red velour of a newborn sleeper and tucked inside my jacket. We took turns steadying Gramps, while others tasted a snowflake or hurled an unexpected snowball.

We slipped and slid our way into the front rows of split-log pews, and released a collective awe as our eyes settled on the stained glass windows of Rocky Mountain wildflowers reflecting a hundred candles' golden glow. We recognized the decorating touches of our mother in the smell of pine and red ribbons tied to the end of each row. We snuggled together, and none more than I, next to my dad.

When the organ, piano, and trumpet announced, "Oh Come All Ye Faithful," all our voices joined in. There may have been varying flavors and degrees of faith among us, but we recognized and celebrated the great faith of our father. We had come from all over the world to love and be loved, to affirm a life and to celebrate a new life. We had eaten turkey stuffing made with cornbread until our bellies ached and had remembered our manners at a table set with wedding silver and Rothchild's Bird china. Bill had yelled, "Bring in the feet!" and we all had laughed, like always, when Gramps said, "Sure is good grub, Babe." A pinecone had popped in the fireplace, Nan had made sure lamps and candles were lit, stockings were "hung by the chimney with care."

At St. James, the final notes began, "Silent Night, Holy Night..." and a small candle quickened near the altar. Quietly, the light began to pass between us. As we leaned in to shelter the flame, we were aware of the warmth of one already lit in our souls. We looked into the eyes of the one next to us—a brother, a neighbor, a child, a dad—and passed on our memories, our hearts, and our hope.

"All is calm, all is bright…" It is so. Let it be so. Come, Lord Jesus. Come Emmanuel.

YOUR OWN RED DIRT OR OLD CABIN STORY

Made in the USA
San Bernardino, CA
07 December 2012